SOUL LANGUAGE:

Consciously Connecting With Your Soul for Success

ABOUT THE AUTHOR

Jennifer Urezzio specializes in helping people connect—to themselves, to each other, and to the Divine. She founded a new paradigm, **Soul Language,** which provides guidance for understanding our true nature and tools for accessing deeper levels of awareness. This new insight into how the Soul expresses itself is being embraced by top healers, lifestyle coaches and CEOs all over the world as a method for helping people recognize their purpose and live from a place of power and truth.

Jennifer was born and raised in New York. Her early career was in corporate America as a media relations specialist. In 2007 she decided to follow her Soul's calling and began showing people how to use Soul Language as a tangible tool to better understand who they are, develop their intuitive abilities, and heal through their own insight. Jennifer now lives in New Jersey and travels to meet with members of the Soul Language community. She speaks professionally and offers classes, workshops, and private consultations, both in person and online. Her personal Soul Languages are *Equalizer (AQ), Teacher of Integrity (AT)*, and *Graceful Warrior (Tone)*. The Soul Languages of her business are *Counselor (AQ), Heart Conscious (AT)*, and *Collaborator (Tone)*. For more information, visit **www.SoulLanguage.us**.

To Write to the Author

If you would like to contact the author, please write your letter in care of "A Good Steward" and we will forward your request. Both the author and publisher welcome your feedback about this book and how it has helped you. A Good Steward will forward your letter, however we cannot guarantee that all letters to the author will be answered. Please write to:

Jennifer Urezzio
c/o A Good Steward
P.O. Box 101
Stirling, NJ 07980

Please enclose a self-addressed, stamped envelope for reply. For more information and resources, visit our website at http://agoodsteward.net.

Jennifer Urezzio

SOUL LANGUAGE:
Consciously Connecting With Your Soul for Success

A Good Steward

Stirling, NJ

First Edition
First Printing, 2013

Edited by Glenn Poole
Cover design by Daniel Yeager

A Good Steward is a registered trademark of A Good Steward LLC.

Library of Congress Cataloguing-in-Publication Data for *Soul Language: Consciously Connecting With Your Soul for Success* is pending.

A Good Steward LLC does not participate in, endorse, or have any authority or responsibility concerning private business transactions between its authors and the public.

All mail addressed to the author is forwarded but the publisher cannot, unless specifically instructed by the author, disclose a mailing address or telephone number.

Any internet references contained in this work are current at publication time, but the publisher cannot guarantee that a specific location will continue to be maintained. Please refer to the publisher's website for links to authors' websites and other sources.

A Good Steward LLC
P.O. Box 101
Stirling, NJ 07980
www.agoodsteward.net

Printed in the United States of America

ACKNOWLEDGMENTS

My path in life is to be a "Faith Seeker." It has been an interesting one so far and I will assume, as time goes on and a deeper connection continues to form, that my path will continue to be interesting.

No path is traveled alone. Although I believe that I have acknowledged these individuals during the trials and tribulations, as well as during the celebrations, I feel it is important to pause and thank them once again in writing.

My heart is filled with a deep gratitude for all the teachers and mentors I have met along the path, and with special thanks to:

God
Baeth Davis
Domenica Papalia
Erin Saxton
Kathy Smyly Miller
Linda Urezzio
Linda Hunt
My Soul
Raymond Urezzio
R.J. Urezzio

For their assistance with editing the Soul Language definitions and the rest of this book with such care, I'd like to thank Glenn Poole, Kathy Smyly Miller, Barb Flynn, Deb Cooperman, Alice Braga, Alissa Okrent, and Jennifer Bloome.

I'd also like to thank all the Soul Language community members for your trust and your commitment to living more consciously. Your Soulful inquiry inspires me, and I am honored to serve as your journey unfolds.

CONTENTS

FOREWORD

By Kathy Smyly Miller

I first heard about Soul Language during a walk in the woods with my dear friend, Janet StraightArrow. Janet had already been a spiritual teacher and intuitive healer for a number of years when she had her Soul Languages identified. As we walked she shared how much this information had helped her. The conversation would move on and then circle back around again. It was obvious that the experience had made an impact, and I made a mental note to investigate further.

Two weeks later I was at lunch with Jennifer Urezzio. By the time we finished dessert, it was clear that I too would have my Soul Languages identified.

The process was conducted over the phone. First my Axiom of Quest (mission Language) was revealed: *Pioneer*. That made sense to me—as any of my family members or friends could have told you, I am always trying new things. Next, my Axiom of Translation: *Purveyor* (how you fuel your mission Language). Yes, I could easily see that people turned to me when they needed a resource. Finally, my Tone (how your Soul sings; you can read more about this in the Tone chapter) was revealed to be *Investigator*. I did not like what I heard, didn't feel convinced and noticed that I wanted to ask if the muscle testing could be done again. Finally I noticed the irony in the fact that I wanted to pursue further investigation.

Over the next few months I had many "Aha!" moments:

I no longer needed to find my purpose. It was already clear, and I had been on purpose all along.

I no longer felt "wrong" about moving from one thing to another, always looking ahead. I came to understand that this is my nature, something God did on purpose.

I saw how I was living the unconscious (shadow side) definition of my Axiom of Translation, "begging, borrowing, or stealing to ensure that other people's needs are met." Letting go of that behavior took a huge load off my back.

I began to enjoy the process of making connections which had always been a habit anyway, now seeing how it could really serve me and others. That initial phone call to Jen was also a natural expression of the *Purveyor* Language as I tapped into another available resource. I began to see how so often I would jump to providing a resource or suggesting one before anyone had even asked, and I made it a new habit to give people a choice: "Would you be interested in a resource that could help you with that?"

My clients and community members appreciated the changes they saw in me and soon had their own Languages identified. This allowed me to see what particular Languages I had attracted, and I was able to get a better sense of how I could serve.

With all this going on, the biggest wake-up call of all happened by getting to know the *Investigator*. This part of me acted like a little girl who had been locked in the closet. Timid and shy, feeling as if no one wanted to see her pretty face, I was expressing the Tone unconsciously and having "attachment to what others do with the information you present to them from your investigations." There were many experiences where my investigations had made people uncomfortable, especially when things were uncovered that they hadn't wanted to see.

It is difficult to put into words how incredibly powerful it can be to accept an aspect of yourself at this deep level. Our familiarity with parts of ourselves that we don't find acceptable turns from shadow to light. Suddenly what we felt made us undesirable becomes our most amazing gift–to ourselves and to humanity.

Jen and I stayed in touch and I found myself drawn to learn more and share with others about this tool for self awareness and self-study. My friends started accepting themselves at a deeper level and I delighted in how much fun we all had just playing and being ourselves fully. We knew what we could rely on each other for and celebrated our uniqueness.

When the opportunity came to be part of the Soul Language movement, I saw how perfectly matched to my particular set of Languages this was. My *Pioneer* was happy to lead the way and experience something new. My *Purveyor* felt supported by the awareness of a metaphysical support team, which had always been there but now could be called upon consciously. My *Investigator* had much to do with getting to know others in the community and seeing how they were working with their Soul Languages.

Then came the opportunity to work on this book. Jen moves quickly through life lessons and challenges, so I often had to run to catch up. Then there were times that I was keenly aware of what was ahead, and Jen welcomed insight about the vision I had for how this information could be shared with the world.

There were specific challenges with this project:

-   Language definitions had been downloaded from Source and some could only be understood by someone with that particular Language. It is true of all the Languages that the definition can only be fully comprehended by someone who speaks that Language, and it is a lifelong process of discovery to see how that Language gets expressed in an individual life. The task was to shape the definitions so that we can all learn about each other by reading them.

-   Working with the material triggered awakenings that had to be integrated in order to move forward with the project.

-   Until now not much has been known about the Soul. While the information seems esoteric, it is actually quite practical and has to be presented in a way that people at all levels of consciousness or stages of awareness can accept and make use of it.

I have loved every minute of this challenge and feel gratitude for all those who have played with me so far in this adventure. I have thoroughly enjoyed working with Jen, even when she "gets a little Warrior" on me as she calls it. Thanks, Jen, for always moving so quickly into the graceful part of the *Graceful Warrior*. I am humbled by the size and scope of the project that was dropped into your lap, and I am honored to participate.

I also had the distinct pleasure and honor of working with my son, Glenn Poole, on this project. As an editor Glenn is an ace, and I admire the way he moved through these challenges to complete the project. In order to remain objective, Glenn chose to wait to have his Soul Languages identified until the project is complete. Glenn, I look forward to having language to describe the gifts and talents I see you sharing in all areas of your life.

Thanks to all the members of the Soul Language community who said "Yes!" to "Soul dates" and allowed me to investigate.

It is my wish for you that you are able to use this book to know yourself better and to feel more connected to others and God.

Kathy Smyly Miller

A Letter from the Founder of Soul Language

Dear Soul Language Community Member:

If you told me a dozen years ago that I would guide a movement for people to consciously connect to their Souls, I think I would have laughed it off (and silently or Soulfully agreed with you).

Soul Language was Divinely downloaded when I was seeking an answer from the Universe to one big, multi-layered question: How can I receive more community interested in what I am interested in? How can I connect deeply with myself and others?

As so often when you request something from the Divine, I received a response. Since then, Soul Language has been helping people connect to their Souls and each other. Soul Language provides tangibility to the intangible so you can recognize, embrace, and be the truth of who you are–love and a Divine expression.

Soul Language is one way you can remember who you are and establish a conscious connection with your Soul.

This process can be combined with all sacred practices. It is a tool for knowing your life purpose and so much more. Understanding your Soul Languages gives you the structure to gain clarity and know, in every fiber of your being, your truth, your message for yourself and others, and your path to Divinely inspired action.

My journey has been an interesting one. It all started by asking God how I could live and be my life purpose. The answer was this body of work. I still remember the moment when I firmly accepted that, in sharing this work, I wasn't insane—that it was a real tool that would support others.

It came when I was identifying a friend's Language. She knew nothing about Soul Language or the Language definitions. After I identified her Language as a *Partner* (Axiom of Translation), she expressed this statement: Before our session I asked myself what would I say if Jennifer asked me what my Soul Language was, and I wrote down the word Partner. Her response was met with tears and the words, thank you for telling me I'm not crazy.

I am keenly aware of how sometimes I created bumps in the road where it could have been more easily paved. One of the biggest hurdles was letting go of individuals who were not ready to go deeper into their connection, even when I could see the possibilities for them. Another was using my courage and strength, not as a way to separate myself from others, but as a resource to build my life and surrender to the Divine.

I am also aware that I am just the beginning of this work, that others will pave different and bigger roads.

I thank you for your participation in Soul Language. Every identification and every practitioner adds to Soul Language, making Soul Language the living and breathing movement that it is.

So be conscious, be connected, be Soulful, and be successful—for that is your true nature.

With love, honor, and gratitude,

Jennifer Urezzio

The Founder and Spiritual Director of Soul Language

P.S. If you have not yet had your Soul Languages identified, I invite you to visit www. SoulLanguage.us. There you can schedule a complimentary discovery session, a 15 minute phone call with a certified Soul Language practitioner who will identify one of your 3 Soul Languages.

PART ONE

Your Soul Speaks

CHAPTER 1:

Meet Your Soul

You will learn in this chapter:

- What is Soul Language?

- Why is it important?

- Where did it come from?

Introduction–What is Soul Language?

For centuries people have been on an expedition to find out who they are, why they are here, and what it all means. Soul Language gives people the tools to answer these questions in an accessible, relatable way. Soul Language is the expression of your true self and your essence. Your Soul contains the agenda of why you are here and what you have to accomplish. Soul Language is the way we communicate that agenda. It's how we think, speak, feel, relate, and express ourselves in the world.

Soul Language is the key that teaches individuals how to participate consciously in their lives. We have the opportunity to consciously connect with our Souls, to let go of old patterns and beliefs, to stop taking negative experiences so personally, and to start enjoying life more fully. This book is a resource to help you do just that.

What's truly amazing about Soul Language is that it's always been there, since we came into this world. That's why this information is so easy to understand and simple to utilize: it's innate in each one of us.

Currently 107 different Soul Languages have been identified. Each and every person has three Soul Languages that he/she speaks. I refer to my three Languages as my Soul Language Team.

Soul Languages fall into three different categories: Axiom of Quest, Axiom of Translation, and Tone. These categories will be explained more in the next chapter.

By understanding your own three Languages, the Languages of others, and the Soul Languages of your business, you will be able to:

- Raise your vibration

- Create healthy relationships

- Create support teams that actually support you

- Create and participate in opportunities of abundance and miracles

- Live Soulfully and accept the power of being yourself

In addition to understanding your three Soul Languages, you will learn to:

- Create your own individual action plan for personal and professional transformation

- Express yourself without conflict

- Attract individuals who speak one of your Languages

- Attract individuals who speak a Soul Language that will help you fulfill or achieve an intention or strategy (goal)

Why is Soul Language important?

The Universe has provided us with tools to understand, accept, and unconditionally love ourselves–Soul Language is one of those tools. You are already using your Soul Languages every second of the day. When you unconsciously use your Soul Languages or fight against them, you create struggle in your life. Struggle takes many forms. It can look like not having enough, it can feel like being stuck, or it can take the form of depression, anger, or resentment, among other things.

As you begin to consciously use the information from your Soul Languages, you become more able to accept who you are and create more powerful, positive experiences. Our physical world is a representation of our inner world. Unconditionally loving yourself is a way to experience more pleasure in the physical world. Soul Language is a powerful tool for accessing guidance and unconditional love within ourselves.

Soul Language also allows us to see how we are all connected. You can use the Soul Language information to find others who share at least one of your Languages: Axiom of Quest, Axiom of Translation, or Tone.

When you connect with someone with whom you share one or more Soul Languages, several things happen:

- You feel connected

- You feel understood

- You share insight and knowledge

- You move faster in your mission

- You understand better how your Soul speaks to you and to others

- You get support in experiencing your greatest desires

When people who share one or more Languages get together they work as amplifiers for each other, and this allows you to more quickly and gracefully achieve your goals. See Chapter 8 for more information about amplification.

Where does the Soul Language information come from?

The Soul Language material and programs were provided to me via Source guidance and inspiration.

I asked the Universe in 2007: "How can I attract more like-minded individuals that I feel connected to? How can I create the life I desire?" The answer from Source was Soul Language. I have been asking additional questions ever since and Soul Language remains a living, breathing movement.

The information is always being updated and new information is always being provided.

Through this information and by consciously using my Soul Languages, my life and the lives of others have been forever transformed.

How does one have their Soul Languages Identified?

Soul Languages are identified using a form of muscle testing called Therapeutic Kinesiology. Rather than asking questions about the person, a Certified Soul Language Practitioner will request permission to establish an energetic connection. Once permission is granted and the energetic connection has been established, the Practitioner will employ muscle testing to determine the client's Soul Language(s).

CHAPTER 2:

The Three Categories of Soul Language

You will learn in this chapter:

- The definition of the Axiom of Quest
- The definition of the Axiom of Translation
- The definition of Tone

The Language Categories

There are 3 categories of Soul Languages and they are all of equal importance. There is no hierarchy within your Soul or within the Soul Language community. It is your specific combination of Languages that makes you so unique.

As an example, you may get excited when you meet someone who has the same birthday as you. Soul Language shows us we are much more unique than that, though. With 19 Axioms of Quest, 33 Axioms of Translation, and 55 Tones, there is a 1 in 34,485 chance that the next person you meet will share all 3 Languages with you. You might go your whole life without ever meeting someone who shares all 3 Languages.

Axiom of Quest

Humans like to KNOW exactly what they are doing, what the strategy is and what their game-plan is. From literature and philosophy to hobbies and careers, we are always trying to figure out WHY we are HERE.

The Axiom of Quest is a person's mission during their lifetime. It's the "why" we are here, our purpose. This category is a driving force behind an individual's Soul in this lifetime, and people often feel as if they need to complete this mission.

Your mission is innately part of your physical, mental, emotional and spiritual makeup. You have been doing your mission without even knowing it since you decided to enter this world. This is the Soul Language that most people feel unaware of…and yet once they hear what it is, there is always a kind of "aha!" moment of recognition.

Having a conscious definition of your mission allows you to actively co-create with your Soul to conduct this mission with fewer struggles.

What we mean by co-creating with the Soul is that you don't try to control it. Your Soul has a master plan. Before you entered this body, you had already decided certain Soul choices. These choices together form a master plan, your Soul's agenda. But you can and do make choices for how each step of this plan gets fulfilled. Struggle comes from making free-will choices that are not in alignment with Soul choices. For example, we may know that the Soulful choice in a relationship is to create a boundary, but then we might ignore that boundary out of fear.

When you consciously understand what your mission is, it becomes your umbrella in any storm. That mission can provide great comfort because it means you have a purpose. Purpose gives you the strength to weather many challenges.

According to Soul Language, your mission will never be completed. The mission is more like a journey than a destination–it is the path. You have been on your mission since the moment you were conceived. Understanding and bringing consciousness to this mission allows you to:

- Be more aligned with your mission

- Receive resources to make the journey without struggle

- Feel like you are fulfilling the mission

- Accept your power and talents

- Be more confident

- Recognize the next step more easily

- Avoid bumps on the path

Axiom of Translation

Just as we each have our own path in life, we also have our own way of being on that path. Even if two people have the same Axiom of Quest, the same mission, they may have different ways of approaching it. Your Axiom of Translation is how you approach your mission; it describes the tools and talents you bring to your life through your Soul.

The Axiom of Translation also describes how you will be known here. Think of the words other people use to describe you; chances are, they are tapping into your Axiom of Translation without even knowing it. One example is the *Weight Carrier*. People with this Language are often described as reliable and strong. They use their strength to help others weather any storm as they move forward in their life purpose.

As you understand your Axiom of Translation more fully, you receive more guidance for the individual steps or expression of your Soul agenda.

Understanding and bringing consciousness to this Language allows you to:

- Be Divinely guided in the "how" of things

- Let go of limiting beliefs that are preventing you from experiencing life without struggle

- Understand and accept your talents in a deeper way

- Receive more guidance about the next steps on your journey

Tone

Your Tone is your Soul's personality in the consciousness of love and without judgment. The way I heard this from the Divine is "It is called the Tone because it is the way your Soul sings. It's the voice of your Soul." Understanding the Tone can provide you with information about your Soul's preferences. Imagine expressing your likes, dislikes, wants, and desires without fear, doubt, or confusion.

Some of us favor combining both the mind and the heart (*Intellect*) while others choose to be at the center of the action (*Ringmaster*).

The Tone is the most likely Soul Language through which ego will be expressed. Understanding and bringing consciousness to this Language allows you to:

- Take things a lot less personally

- Be more compassionate for yourself and for others

- Live more courageously

These categories will be explained further in Part Two.

CHAPTER 3:

Expressing Your Soul Languages

You will learn in this chapter:

- The difference between "conscious" and "unconscious" in Soul Language

- The definition of free-will in Soul Language:

- How Soul Languages can be still or action-oriented

The difference between conscious and unconscious in Soul Language:

We've seen how Soul Languages are divided into three different categories. Every individual on this planet speaks one Language from each of the three different categories. These are your Languages for this lifetime, and they do not change during your life here on this planet.

But even if you speak the same Soul Language as another person, because of the particular combination of your Soul Languages and your personal experiences, you bring a unique expression to each Language.

We each use our Languages in a conscious way (without judgment/Soulful) or unconscious way (in judgment/shadow).

We will define conscious use of the Languages as:

- Unconditional love, without judgment for one's self

- Self-acceptance

- In alignment with body, mind, and spirit

- In light

We will define unconscious use of the Languages as:

- Conditional, with judgment for one's self

- Self denial or self criticism

- Out of alignment with body, mind, and spirit

- In shadow

Each Language description includes examples of when an individual is expressing their Soul Language consciously or unconsciously.

A couple of points on using your Languages unconsciously:

You can be unaware of a judgment that you are holding with regard to an aspect of yourself. You can also become aware of a judgment and any resistance to letting go of that judgment.

Please understand that you can be accepting of yourself on one level and still be in judgment on a deeper level.

When an individual acts without the consciousness of love, for example by making choices with conditions, this generates a misalignment with the Soul that results in disharmony and unhappiness in that individual.

Understanding Free-Will Choices:

A suggested metaphor for free will is this: Source knows everything that is going to happen if you go left on the path, and Source knows everything that is going to happen if you go right on the path, but Source doesn't know whether you are going to go right or left.

Language Orientation

Each Soul Language falls into one of three orientations: Action, Still or Action/Still. This describes how the Language first reacts. For example:

- Action-Oriented Languages will desire to react with action

- Still-Oriented Languages will first become introspective or retreat for information

- The Action/Still-Oriented Languages look for a balanced approach between reflection and immediate action

Depending on the Soul Languages a person has, their Action or Still orientations may become more Action or more Still as a result of that specific combination.

PART TWO

Getting to Know Your Soul

CHAPTER 4:

Connecting to Your Languages

You will learn in this chapter how to:

- Read your Language definitions

- Create a conscious connection with your Soul Languages

- Collaborate with your Soul Languages

Components of the Soul Language Definition

First, the most important thing to remember is that Soul Language is a living and breathing movement: the Language definitions are being updated with more information every day. These definitions are a starting point for you to have a conscious conversation with your Soul.

In receiving information from the Divine, sometimes it doesn't look or sound like we "think" it should look or sound.

I would also like to take a moment to explain the different parts of each definition and provide additional insight on how the information is presented.

Please keep in mind that you might read a Language definition that is not your own and is not completely clear to you. This is understandable because the Language definitions are written to be clear for those who share that Language.

In compiling the book, the editors have toiled to preserve the Divinely guided definition while presenting the simplest and clearest explanation.

Following is a breakdown with a brief description of the parts of the Language definitions.

Description

The first section of each definition provides a brief explanation of the Language's expression. Please keep in mind that Soul Language is always evolving and expanding, so it is safe to say that these descriptions will keep evolving over time.

We are trying to put structure and tangibility to Soul. We are using human words to talk about something indescribable. No description is intended to place you in a box, to pigeonhole you, or to tell you who you are.

Influential Words

Humans like words. When we have put a name to something we seem to connect to it on a deeper level. This section of the definition is to inspire, guide, support, and allow for a deeper connection to your Soul Language. We have noticed people relating to these words, using these words to describe themselves and including the influential words in marketing pieces.

Abilities & Talents

We have a habit of undervaluing talents that come easily and gracefully to us. The section on "talents" is to highlight the natural abilities of the parts of your Soul; this will allow you to accept these talents and embrace the expression of these gifts for yourself and for others.

Consciously or Unconsciously experiencing your Languages

These sections are to allow you to become aware of how you are focusing your Soulful energy. Being in the conscious use of your Language will more than likely result in feelings of connection and a sense of being in the flow. Being in the unconscious use of your Language will more than likely result in feeling disconnected, unsupported, and out of alignment.

Signs you are on the path

Humans tend to love lists. The "Signs you are on the path" section is a Soulful checklist that supports you in recognizing the conscious use of your Languages. When you are using your Language consciously, you will notice these signs.

Language Orientation

Each Language falls into one of three orientations: Action, Still, or Action/Still. This describes how the Language first reacts. For example, an Action-oriented Language will desire an action step first while a Still-oriented one will first go inside or retreat for information.

The Action/Still classification allows for a balanced effect to happen. Depending on the makeup of the Languages, the Action/Still Language can be more Still or more Action-oriented.

Accessing and Attracting Support

Resources that we have been praying for usually find their way to us via other human beings. In this day and age we crave connection and community. Soul Language supports the fulfillment of this desire by giving us insight about what we have to offer others, and about what others have to offer us. This part of the definition has specific examples of how particular Soul Languages can support you.

Conscious Business

Your business has an essence, it has a Soul. From a Soulful perspective, we create a business to do something for ourselves and for others in a bigger way. This takes additional energy. This section is to help provide insight on what awareness is needed if you have a business that "speaks" that Language.

A Soul Language identification for a business can be conducted with permission from the owner(s).

Conscious Parenting

It is an amazing gift for both parent and child when a parent knows their child's Soul Languages. It allows them to recognize and nurture unique talents and honor their child's Soulful expression. It also allows the parent to receive the gifts that child is bringing into their life.

A Soul Language identification for a child can be conducted with permission from the parent.

This section can be utilized two different ways. The first use is to guide parents in supporting their child who speaks that Language. The second way is for the adult to provide the child inside with resources that were not received during childhood.

Questions

This section is to provide you the opportunity to be in conversation with your Soul. These questions are starter questions and will lead to your own questions.

Reading Your Language Definitions

Here is the suggested process for reading your Language definitions:

- Read your definition over once to get an idea of the big picture and your mission

- Read the material again more closely, allowing the information and your Languages to speak to you on a deeper level

- Create a conscious connection with your Soul; try imagining that part of you is seated across the table from you, or just set the intention to connect with your Soul

- Begin reading the conscious and unconscious expressions of the Language again, being aware of how those expressions may be showing up in your life

- Ask this part of your Soul the questions provided and any others that come to you; be open to hearing, seeing, or feeling the answers

- Take notes and continue rereading the definition to explore further

- Connect with your Language(s) every day to maintain your conscious connection, continue the conversation, and listen to guidance

Creating a Conscious Connection with Your Soul Languages

To understand yourself more fully and deeply, you can start by listening to the wisdom of your Soul. By creating a conscious connection with yourself and your Soul Languages, your mind will have a way to access deep information and knowledge. Please keep in mind that this connection is always available. When we place some structure around it, however, it sets up a sacred space which allows us to be present and mindful.

Here are two ways to create a conscious connection. Both start by taking a deep breath and allowing your awareness to focus on your tailbone. Focusing on your tailbone allows your Soul to be more firmly anchored in your body, which some people describe as feeling "grounded". Throughout the book, the phrase "creating a conscious connection" refers to this process.

Option A–Visualization

Imagine your Soul Language Team Member (this is one of your Soul Languages) sitting across from you, looking eye-to-eye. If you wish to speak to all three of your Soul Languages at the same time, imagine all three of them sitting across the table from you.

Option B–Intention Setting

Simply ask Divine Intelligence to establish a conscious working connection between you and the Soul Language Team Member you wish to connect with. Once you have requested this connection, trust that it is in place.

After you are finished with your meditation or conversation, thank your Soul Languages, yourself, and your higher power. Then release the conscious connection by saying: *I release this conscious working connection.*

Collaborating with Your Soul Languages

There are several ways to connect with your Soul to create the life you desire. Below are several suggestions.

Insight Questions

After you connect to your Soul Language Team Member, ask the questions provided in the individual Soul Language definition or create your own questions. Then spend a few minutes journaling about the responses you receive. Responses may be sensations, feelings, thoughts, memories, visions, or even indescribable experiences.

Intention Setting

What's your intention for today? When we declare our intention, it allows the Universe to create on our behalf. Your intention is not a "to-do" list. It is a way to fuel your life with positive energy, and to attract positive experiences. Try setting your intention with a focus on how you want to feel. Here's an example: "Today I intend to feel peaceful, prosperous, and full of life."

Create a conscious connection with your Soul Language Team and complete the sentence below:

My personal intention for today is...

Want to add additional power to your intention? Write it down in your journal and say it aloud.

Conversation

After you create a conscious connection, begin a conversation with your Soul Language Team Members. Explore what is currently happening in your life or a situation that you would like some support and guidance for. If you get stuck wondering where to start, refer to the questions included in the individual Soul Language definitions as a jumping-off point.

CHAPTER 5:

Axiom of Quest – Being Your Mission

You will learn in this chapter:

- The different Axioms of Quest

- How to collaborate with your Axiom of Quest

- Questions for your Axiom of Quest

Axiom of Quest

Your Axiom of Quest is your mission during your lifetime. Your purpose is what you are here to experience and share with others. It's a source of both great joy and great challenge. Your mission can come so easily and effortlessly that you may not recognize the value and the profound impact this Language has on you and others. In fact, most individuals are under the impression that their mission is about "doing" something, and this results in confusion.

In understanding your Axiom of Quest, you can have a deeper knowledge of the elements of your journey. For example, a *Mentor's* journey will always be about self-mentoring first and then sharing that experience by mentoring others.

Collaborating With Your Axiom of Quest

Understanding and bringing consciousness to this Language allows you to:

- Be more aligned with this mission

- Receive resources to allow the journey to be without struggle

- Feel like you are fulfilling the mission

- Accept your power and talents

- Be more confident

- Recognize the next step on the path more easily

- Avoid bumps on the path

Intention Setting

Create a conscious connection with your Axiom of Quest and complete the sentence below:

My personal intention for my path today is...

Want to add additional power to your intention? Write it down in your journal and say it out loud.

Questions for Your Axiom of Quest

Create a conscious connection with your Axiom of Quest. Then ask these questions to initiate a conversation with your Axiom of Quest:

What do I get to accept, allow, activate or let go of that will help me be more aligned with my mission and create the life that I desire?

What action can I take today that will allow me to feel and be more aligned with my purpose?

How can I be more aligned with this mission?

How can I open up to receiving resources to allow the journey to be without struggle?

What are some triggers that make me feel as if I'm not on the mission or living my purpose?

How can I tap into talents I may be unaware of?

How can I access and express my personal power more?

What does confidence feel like in my body? How can I express confidence more fully?

What is the next Divinely inspired action on my path?

What am I holding onto that is no longer serving me or my path?

For additional questions see the definition of your Axiom of Quest.

Axiom of Quest Language Definitions

There are 19 Languages in this category. As you understand your Axiom of Quest more fully you will become clear about your mission, your purpose for this lifetime.

Sometimes after an individual has their Axiom of Quest identified, they will look through the other Languages in this category and judge their Language. Once you let go of the judgment and embrace your mission, you will understand that no other decision could have been made for you. Each of us inherently knows our purpose here, and the journey of life is to express it.

AMBASSADOR

Axiom of Quest

Your mission is to be a bridge of love and understanding and to illustrate benevolent cooperation for yourself and others.

You have specific talents which you utilize to advise and assist yourself and others with creating balance and harmony between opposing parties.

INFLUENTIAL WORDS:

Collaboration

Bridge

Communication

ABILITIES AND TALENTS:

You understand how love can be a bridge between any two parties

You can tap into Divine wisdom to understand how to create a bridge for cooperation

CONSCIOUSLY EXPERIENCING THIS LANGUAGE:

Tapping into the Universe's Divine wisdom to create this bridge for yourself and others

Embracing love as the guiding force for cooperation

Engaging with parties that are willing to have a dialogue and cooperate

Understanding that not everyone wants to be in balance and harmony

Knowing what you desire in order to have balance and harmony in your own life

Creating and maintaining clear boundaries

UNCONSCIOUSLY EXPERIENCING THIS LANGUAGE:

Refusing to accept that you are a channel for the Universe's love and inspiration

Having inappropriate boundaries or no boundaries

Judging yourself and others

Inappropriately communicating or withholding communication of your wants, needs, and desires

Feeling divided and unsupported

Demanding cooperation instead of providing opportunities for creating bridges

Being attached to what you are offering

SIGNS YOU ARE ON THE PATH:

You are full of love and compassion for yourself

You know what you need for balance and harmony

LANGUAGE ORIENTATION:

The *Ambassador* is Still. Your Soul has a desire to reflect prior to taking action. The key for the *Ambassador* is to allow this reflection to take place without getting so caught up in the stillness that no action is taken.

ACCESSING AND ATTRACTING SUPPORT:

Avatar (Axiom of Quest) – These individuals each embody a belief or principle. They can help the *Ambassador* be more loving and compassionate.

Master (Axiom of Translation) – These are the big idea people. They can help the *Ambassador* understand the big picture in order to create more opportunities for cooperation.

Developer (Tone) – These individuals are investors by nature. They can help the *Ambassador* see opportunities for expansion. This information can help the *Ambassador* explain the common ground between individuals so collaboration can take place.

IF YOUR BUSINESS'S AXIOM OF QUEST IS AMBASSADOR:

You are clear about what the company needs to be in balance

You use love to motivate clients, employees, and your community

You understand what bridges you are creating and for who

A CHILD WHO SPEAKS THIS LANGUAGE WILL THRIVE IN AN ENVIRONMENT THAT:

Provides them with a secure sense of self

Provides them with a deep sense of faith

Provides structures to create balance and harmony

QUESTIONS TO ASK YOUR AMBASSADOR:

Where can I create balance and harmony in my life?

Where am I lacking in communication with others, with myself, or with the Divine?

Arranger

Axiom of Quest

Your mission is to put things in their proper order for the benefit of all. Even chaos has an order and rhythm to it.

You group, categorize, plan, organize, and give order to objects, beliefs, people, communities, etc. to serve a larger cause.

Influential words:

Assemble

Order

Sort

Abilities and Talents:

You are able to see the order in everything

You have a keen sense of how to assemble things to bring about a sense of peace

Consciously experiencing this Language:

Understanding that there is no universal template for arranging things

Creating order with both discernment and intuition

Being clear about the strategy you use to create your own order

Being clear that it is not your responsibility to make order out of chaos for others; you just provide opportunities for them to find order for themselves

Understanding the larger purpose of your arranging process

UNCONSCIOUSLY EXPERIENCING THIS LANGUAGE:

Constantly rearranging, never letting go and allowing things to organize themselves

Feeling overwhelmed

Feeling as if you can't get it all done

Constantly arranging things for others while avoiding your own life

Forcing others to arrange for your own purposes, not allowing for free-will choices

SIGNS YOU ARE ON THE PATH:

You understand what needs arranging in your own life and world

You understand your mission or cause

LANGUAGE ORIENTATION:

The *Arranger* is Action. Your Soul has a desire to move directly into action. If you don't find balance and discernment in your actions, you could feel like you are on a hamster wheel.

ACCESSING AND ATTRACTING SUPPORT:

Caretaker (Axiom of Quest) – These individuals take care of a belief, theory, group, or object. They can help the *Arranger* to understand their larger cause.

Goddess (Axiom of Translation) – These individuals are accepting of their Divine feminine nature. They can help the *Arranger* to balance their male and female energies.

Ark Builder (Tone) – These individuals see a totally different way of approaching the "how" of things. They can help the *Arranger* understand better how things can fall into place.

IF YOUR BUSINESS'S AXIOM OF QUEST IS ARRANGER:

You are clear about what is being arranged for others

You have clear boundaries for yourself and respect the boundaries of others

You are clear about the larger cause or mission and you communicate it effectively

A CHILD WHO SPEAKS THIS LANGUAGE WILL THRIVE IN AN ENVIRONMENT THAT:

Provides them with clear boundaries

Allows them to play

Provides opportunities to notice when they are overwhelmed and tools for processing those feelings

QUESTIONS TO ASK YOUR ARRANGER:

Why am I arranging this situation in my life?

What am I trying to arrange that is not mine to organize?

AVATAR

Axiom of Quest

Your mission is to be a living embodiment of a faith or principal. You are all about "walking the talk."

You are able to take esoteric concepts like faith, religion, God, etc. and put them into words that everyone can understand and choose whether to accept in their own lives. You are able to act as the role model for this idea, belief, or faith.

Some famous *Avatars* were Jesus, the Dalai Lama, and Karl Marx.

INFLUENTIAL WORDS:

Love

Compassion

Faith

ABILITIES AND TALENTS:

You are able to explain the esoteric so others can understand and integrate it to improve their lives

You have inside you the capacity for deep love for yourself and others

CONSCIOUSLY EXPERIENCING THIS LANGUAGE:

Having a clear sense of balance between the Divine and humanity

Being a balanced tool for love, compassion, forgiveness, and peace

Walking your talk

Being unafraid to speak your truth, and yet not forcing this truth on anyone

Expressing the consciousness of love and forgiveness for yourself and others

Feeling grounded in both Soul and body

Unconsciously experiencing this Language:

Being mired in counter-productive behaviors or expressing ego-driven emotions

Using your beliefs to satisfy your own desire for validation, love, and support

Expressing what is known as the "God Complex"

Being afraid to speak your truth

Living in fear and in judgment

Feeling disconnected from the Divine

Living ungrounded

Signs you are on the path:

You are clear about your own desires and accept them

You are walking your talk

Language Orientation:

The *Avatar* is Action/Still. Your Soul has a desire to reflect prior to moving into action. It is important that you take sacred time for reflection and tune in to receive and act on Divine guidance.

Accessing and Attracting Support:

Counselor (Axiom of Quest) – These individuals provide guidance in a particular area. They can help the *Avatar* better understand themselves and their mission.

Hero (Axiom of Translation) – These individuals can help the *Avatar* feel the courage inside of them to speak their truth.

Ark Builder (Tone) – These individuals can help the *Avatar* work better with the "how" of things in order to help them manifest their desires.

IF YOUR BUSINESS'S AXIOM OF QUEST IS AVATAR:

The mission of the business is clearly conveyed

The business has systems in place to promote balance

The business has a clear compensation structure

A CHILD WHO SPEAKS THIS LANGUAGE WILL THRIVE IN AN ENVIRONMENT THAT:

Provides them with a strong sense of self

Provides opportunities to understand and express their deep compassion for themselves and others

Supports their quest for knowledge of appropriate topics

QUESTIONS TO ASK YOUR AVATAR:

Where am I not embodying my beliefs?

Where can I forgive myself?

BRIDGEWALKER

Axiom of Quest

Your mission is to create or form bridges (spiritual, mental, material, or emotional) of support.

You have an innate ability to construct these bridges or connections for yourself and for others to access improvement, support, and expansion in order to get closer to what the Soul truly desires.

INFLUENTIAL WORDS:

Link

Connection

Support

ABILITIES AND TALENTS:

You have an innate knowing of how to create support

You have the inexhaustible courage to first walk over a bridge and then invite others to follow

CONSCIOUSLY EXPERIENCING THIS LANGUAGE:

Using love to create bridges of support

Understanding where bridges need to be created in your own life and moving across them

Offering bridges to others only after you have crossed them yourself

Understanding and accepting what your Soul truly desires

Connecting the dots to bridge together the Soul's desires and the material world

UNCONSCIOUSLY EXPERIENCING THIS LANGUAGE:

Creating bridges based on fear, leading to undesirable results in your life

Feeling afraid to move forward in your life

Denying your Soul's desires

Feeling paralyzed and unable to see how to create your own bridge

SIGNS YOU ARE ON THE PATH:

You are conscious of what materials you are using to build your bridges (love or fear)

You have your own bridges of support in place

LANGUAGE ORIENTATION:

The *Bridgewalker* is Action. Your Soul has a desire to move directly into creating and taking action. It is important that you act on Divine inspiration or you will take action without creating the desired results.

ACCESSING AND ATTRACTING SUPPORT:

Elemental (Axiom of Quest) – These individuals have a gift in working with the fundamental building blocks of nature. They can help the *Bridgewalker* understand the resources they need to build their bridges.

Gardener (Axiom of Translation) – These individuals are able to help anything grow. They can help the *Bridgewalker* nurture their own gifts and talents.

Agent (Tone) – These individuals are all about Divine action. They can help the *Bridgewalker* understand what Divine action is to be taken.

IF YOUR BUSINESS'S AXIOM OF QUEST IS BRIDGEWALKER:

The company is clear about what support it offers

The company has a clear sense of its goals (desires) and expresses them

The company is willing to cross new bridges

A CHILD WHO SPEAKS THIS LANGUAGE WILL THRIVE IN AN ENVIRONMENT THAT:

Encourages self-acceptance

Provides opportunities to understand the difference between needs, wants, and desires

Provides structure for both action and reflection

QUESTIONS TO ASK YOUR BRIDGEWALKER:

What new bridge of support do I get to create for myself?

What am I afraid of that is preventing me from expanding?

CARETAKER

Axiom of Quest

Your mission is to be the custodian of a belief, theory, person, or thing. Whatever the *Caretaker* is in charge of has a significant impact on the planet, the world, and the Universe.

Your mission is not to add to, develop, or influence the thing you are in charge of…it is truly profound just to be its steward. Your mission is to guard, protect, and care for it on a daily basis.

INFLUENTIAL WORDS:

Protect

Steward

Guardian

ABILITIES AND TALENTS:

You are able to display deep compassion

You are able to see what needs care

CONSCIOUSLY EXPERIENCING THIS LANGUAGE:

Understanding what you are a steward of

Creating relationships that are nurturing and supportive

Having boundaries in place for your caretaking

Being loving toward yourself

Caring for yourself as much as what you take care of

UNCONSCIOUSLY EXPERIENCING THIS LANGUAGE:

Being unaware of what you are a steward of

Creating co-dependent relationships

Believing you need to take care of everything and sacrifice yourself for others

Being a professional victim

SIGNS YOU ARE ON THE PATH:

You take care of yourself

You have created appropriate boundaries for yourself and with others

You have created relationships that are truly supportive and loving

LANGUAGE ORIENTATION:

The *Caretaker* is Action. Your Soul has a desire to move directly into action. This could lead you to create action for the sake of action.

ACCESSING AND ATTRACTING SUPPORT:

Pioneer (Axiom of Quest) – These individuals can teach the *Caretaker* to be comfortable discovering new roads.

Huntress/Hunter (Axiom of Translation) – These individuals can teach the *Caretaker* how to track what they are taking care of, and what direction it may take.

Captain (Tone) – These individuals can help the *Caretaker* stand up for their boundaries.

IF YOUR BUSINESS'S AXIOM OF QUEST IS CARETAKER:

You know what the company is a steward of

You have clear boundaries

You have created appropriate support teams for the company

A CHILD WHO SPEAKS THIS LANGUAGE WILL THRIVE IN AN ENVIRONMENT THAT:

Provides them with distinct boundaries

Provides them with the tools to create truly supportive relationships

Provides them with a structure for communicating with their higher power

QUESTIONS TO ASK YOUR CARETAKER:

Where do I get to take care of myself more?

What am I the custodian of?

Counselor

Axiom of Quest

Your mission is to be an advisor. You provide specific counsel that serves a deliberate purpose, strategy, or design.

You work with others to exchange ideas or opinions and then recommend a course of action for yourself and others.

You provide wisdom and consultation, but you may not have to play an active role in a particular individual's life.

Influential words:

Advice

Guidance

Expertise

Abilities and Talents:

You have a keen sense of what advice or counsel is required

You are able to see what path someone can take to move past their challenges

Consciously experiencing this Language:

Understanding where you need counsel

Looking within for counsel and, when needed, requesting counsel from an outside source

Providing counsel to others without attachment

Listening deeply to yourself or another before providing thoughts, opinions, or expertise

Unconsciously experiencing this Language:

Having an emotional stake in the guidance and advice you are providing

Trying to control or manipulate the outcome of your advice or guidance

Playing an active role in an individual's life, trying to act for them on the advice or guidance you have given

Judging your path or the paths of others

Signs you are on the path:

You know what counsel you require

You are listening deeply to your own counsel

Language Orientation:

The *Counselor* is Action/Still. Your Soul has a desire to reflect. It is important that you embrace the stillness to really determine what needs to be shifted in your own life and to determine if it is appropriate to offer your counsel to another.

Accessing and Attracting Support:

Counselor (Axiom of Quest) – Attracting others like you can help you feel comfortable about asking for additional guidance from outside sources.

Heart Conscious (Axiom of Translation) – These individuals operate based on heart energy. They can help the *Counselor* provide guidance that is based on both the mind and the heart.

Bodybuilder (Tone) – These individuals can help build up form and Soul. They can help the *Counselor* know all the individual parts of a situation and how they impact the whole.

IF YOUR BUSINESS'S AXIOM OF QUEST IS COUNSELOR:

The company provides advice without attachment or judgment

The company has clear boundaries with respect to client relations

The company clearly expresses its expertise, what counsel it is providing, and to whom it is being provided

A CHILD WHO SPEAKS THIS LANGUAGE WILL THRIVE IN AN ENVIRONMENT THAT:

Provides appropriate boundaries

Allows them to cultivate a strong sense of self

Teaches that it is acceptable to ask for and receive help

QUESTIONS TO ASK YOUR COUNSELOR:

Where am I not listening to myself?

Where am I trying to control the outcome?

ELEMENTAL

Axiom of Quest

Your mission is to feel, see, and explain the connection we have with Nature (all of form). You are able to work with the fundamental building blocks of Nature, including air, fire, water, earth, and metal.

INFLUENTIAL WORDS:

Nature

Universe

Co-create

ABILITIES AND TALENTS:

You are able to see how something is created

You are able to work with the building blocks of Nature (earth, air, fire, water and metal)

CONSCIOUSLY EXPERIENCING THIS LANGUAGE:

Being awake to the natural consciousness

Hearing the natural world around you

Working alongside Nature for balance and harmony for all

Communicating and translating for Nature

Understanding the "how" of the Universe

Co-creating with the "how" of the Universe

Understanding what elements require change

Being open to change

UNCONSCIOUSLY EXPERIENCING THIS LANGUAGE:

Experiencing anxiety or stress about how to create or get something done

Denying Nature and your connection to it

Trying to control the "how"

Trying to control Nature

Judging how you do things

Resisting change

SIGNS YOU ARE ON THE PATH:

You are in balance and harmony with your world

You have let go of control and are co-creating with the world

LANGUAGE ORIENTATION:

The *Elemental* is Still. Your Soul has a desire for reflection. This allows you to understand how things are created and to listen to the world of Nature for guidance.

ACCESSING AND ATTRACTING SUPPORT:

Prophet (Axiom of Quest) – These individuals can help the *Elemental* understand what structures belong to what messages in order to see what could be changed to create a better structure.

Nurturer (Axiom of Translation) – These individuals can help the *Elemental* understand what they need to nurture in themselves.

Captain (Tone) – These individuals can share procedures with the *Elemental* that, if put into place, will help to balance change.

Also see the *Guardian* (Tone), page 363.

IF YOUR BUSINESS'S AXIOM OF QUEST IS ELEMENTAL:

You understand the building blocks of the company

You understand the "how" of the company

You are open to course corrections within the company

A CHILD WHO SPEAKS THIS LANGUAGE WILL THRIVE IN AN ENVIRONMENT THAT:

Provides structures for balance

Provides them with ways to connect with Nature

Provides them with appropriate ways to process change

QUESTIONS TO ASK YOUR ELEMENTAL:

How can I work with the "how" better in this situation?

What element do I get to change for myself here?

Equalizer

Axiom of Quest

Your mission is to create a balanced formula for internal sustainability. You are all about restoring equilibrium within yourself, within others, and for the planet.

You have an innate understanding of this concept: if you pick up a stone in one area of the planet, a stone drops somewhere else. You desire fairness, balance, and equality. *Equalizers* also have an innate understanding of how to find the perfect balance for creation and manifestation.

Influential words:

Balance

Equality

Harmony

Abilities and talents:

Your presence will naturally cause situations to come into balance (even if just temporarily)

You can often sense when something or someone is out of balance

Consciously experiencing this Language:

Accepting and living without attachment to a particular outcome

Having a clear understanding of what fair, balanced and equal mean to you; always tuning in to maintain those definitions

Knowing that balance and equality are being restored even if you do not witness it

Maintaining your own balance formula

Knowing and being unafraid to share (when appropriate) how others may know their own balanced formula for a sustainable and joyful life

UNCONSCIOUSLY EXPERIENCING THIS LANGUAGE:

Judging yourself

Thinking that things are unfair or "some people always win"

Judging others for their lack of balance

Ignoring your needs, wants, or desires

SIGNS YOU ARE ON THE PATH:

You have internal and external systems in place for self-care and self-growth

You know your own formula for balance

You have a clear definition of what balance and equality mean to you

LANGUAGE ORIENTATION:

The *Equalizer* is Action/Still. Your Soul has a desire to reflect prior to taking action. Being out of balance could lead you to more stillness or more action than is needed.

ACCESSING AND ATTRACTING SUPPORT:

Counselor (Axiom of Quest) – These individuals can help exchange ideas and provide recommendations that can help *Equalizers* create more conscious balance for themselves and others.

Messenger (Axiom of Translation) – These individuals can help the *Equalizer* be balanced as they transform through life.

Shepherd (Tone) – These individuals can provide the *Equalizer* with additional ways to lead by example.

IF YOUR BUSINESS'S AXIOM OF QUEST IS EQUALIZER:

You understand and maintain the balance between giving and receiving

You understand what balance the business can offer to others

You feel free to share information and have a balanced structure for compensation

A CHILD WHO SPEAKS THIS LANGUAGE WILL THRIVE IN AN ENVIRONMENT THAT:

Provides opportunities to communicate about what they see or sense is out of balance

Provides them with tools to create their own sense of balance and peace

Provides them with a strong sense of self-worth

QUESTIONS TO ASK YOUR EQUALIZER:

Where can I bring more balance to this situation?

What is the reason I'm choosing not to experience the consciousness of love?

GENIUS

Axiom of Quest

Your mission is to usher in a new way of existence, to influence conduct, and to change history, events, and the way people think.

This mission is not about your IQ. It is your innate ability, through the vehicle of Divine intelligence, to be the spark for a movement, a revolution, or a new way of being that changes people, the planet, and the Universe.

INFLUENTIAL WORDS:

Intelligence

Movement

New Way

ABILITIES AND TALENTS:

You have a keen intellect

You are able to see things in new ways

CONSCIOUSLY EXPERIENCING THIS LANGUAGE:

Understanding this intelligence is both within and outside of you (part of you and part of the Universe)

Creating true support teams that help fan the fire of this movement

Feeling and seeing the physical expression of a new way of being

Being open and unconditional to yourself and others

Being unafraid of the "bigness" of your mission

UNCONSCIOUSLY EXPERIENCING THIS LANGUAGE:

Feeling alone and misunderstood

Feeling as if there is no movement in your life or with your mission

Trying to control the process

Being full of pride and self-righteousness

Feeling like a failure

SIGNS YOU ARE ON THE PATH:

You have a regular practice for connecting with the Divine

You experience and express the consciousness of love for yourself

You have created true support teams in your life

LANGUAGE ORIENTATION:

The *Genius* is Still. Your Soul has a desire for reflection. This reflection is a way for you to receive the information to develop the ideas behind a new way of being.

ACCESSING AND ATTRACTING SUPPORT:

Matriarch/Patriarch (Axiom of Quest) – These individuals can help the *Genius* understand how to receive and lead their community.

Lawmaker (Axiom of Translation) – These individuals can help the *Genius* recreate structures to support peace from within.

Conductor (Tone) – These individuals can help the *Genius* understand how to bring together support teams for everyone to perform at their best.

IF YOUR BUSINESS'S AXIOM OF QUEST IS GENIUS:

You have created clear communications on the new way that the company is providing

You have created clear communications on the mission of the company

You have created appropriate support teams for the company

A CHILD WHO SPEAKS THIS LANGUAGE WILL THRIVE IN AN ENVIRONMENT THAT:

Provides them with practices to look within for information

Encourages them to share their insight

Provides them with a strong sense of self

QUESTIONS TO ASK YOUR GENIUS:

Where can I see something new here?

Where can I look within for knowledge?

Gladiator

Axiom of Quest

Your mission is to be the champion of a single cause, concept, or belief.

This cause is created in partnership with the Divine and you are the champion of that cause on this planet.

Influential words:

Divine

Support

Reason

Abilities and Talents:

You have vast courage and strength

You are able to rally support

Consciously experiencing this Language:

Being aware of your Divine cause

Utilizing compassion and grace to champion this Divine cause

Enlisting support for this cause from those around you

Knowing that you have no opponent: in Divine grace there is no opposition

Practicing alert stillness

Feeling filled with Divine passion

Being without attachment

Using Divine love as fuel to support your cause

Unconsciously experiencing this Language:

Feeling held captive by the fight, as if it is consuming you

Misunderstanding the cause you are supporting

Being controversial for the sake of being controversial

Using anger to fuel your support for your cause

Acting like a radical crusader, not allowing others free-will decisions

Feeling like your mission is a burden

Signs you are on the path:

You know your cause

You act without attachment

You are filled with Divine passion and grace without judgment or anger

Language Orientation:

The *Gladiator* is Action/Still. Your Soul has a desire for reflection prior to taking action. This will allow you to understand when to fight with passion or champion through love.

Accessing and Attracting Support:

Mentor (Axiom of Quest) – These individuals can help the *Gladiator* mentor the love inside of them, guiding them to their cause.

Image Maker (Axiom of Translation) – These individuals see the essence of a being and then help bring that essence into reality. They can help the *Gladiator* see past the anger to the love of the Soul and the Divine.

Carter (Tone) – These individuals express a certain message. Everything they feel, do and say is encoded with this message. They can help the *Gladiator* understand that championing their cause doesn't have to be a burden.

IF YOUR BUSINESS'S AXIOM OF QUEST IS GLADIATOR:

You understand the "cause" of the company

You create ties and joint ventures with truly supportive individuals and companies

You know that there is no competition in the world because there is enough for everyone

A CHILD WHO SPEAKS THIS LANGUAGE WILL THRIVE IN AN ENVIRONMENT THAT:

Provides them with tools to champion with love instead of their fists

Provides them with support to learn and understand their cause

Provides them with a strong foundation of faith and love

QUESTIONS TO ASK YOUR GLADIATOR:

What is my cause?

Where do I need support?

Matriarch/Patriarch

Axiom of Quest

Your mission is to be the leader or ruler of a clan or community. You have the authority, life experiences, past life experiences and trustworthiness to lead a clan or community.

Influential words:

Community

Leadership

Power

Abilities and talents:

You know what needs to be done in order to get the job done

You have a deep understanding of what is best for a group or a community

Consciously experiencing this Language:

Attracting your community easily and without effort

Feeling comfortable with your role as a leader

Understanding and embracing leadership qualities

Being balanced in your actions

Setting appropriate boundaries

UNCONSCIOUSLY EXPERIENCING THIS LANGUAGE:

Not trusting yourself or others

Feeling lost, without a community or family

Feeling unsupported

Dictating instead of leading

Being out of balance with male and female energy

Doing and not receiving

Receiving and not doing

SIGNS YOU ARE ON THE PATH:

You feel loved and supported

You accept your role as a leader

You know how to attract your community

LANGUAGE ORIENTATION:

The *Matriarch/Patriarch* is Action/Still. Your Soul has a desire to reflect prior to taking action. It is important as a leader to be in the stillness so you truly understand the appropriate action to take. If you are out of balance in Action/Still you will feel unsupported by your community.

ACCESSING AND ATTRACTING SUPPORT:

Observer (Axiom of Quest) – The *Observer's* mission is to record, observe, and report. They can help the *Matriarch/Patriarch* understand their history and the history of others in order to be a better leader.

Sitting Buddha (Axiom of Translation) – These individuals will be known here for their ability to be comfortable and enjoy the stillness. They will be able to guide the *Matriarch/Patriarch* in being comfortable with the stillness and creating a deeper connection with the Divine.

Capitalist (Tone) – These individuals prefer to go through life creating prosperity and abundance in order to produce more prosperity and abundance. They can help the *Matriarch/Patriarch* create safety for money and abundance.

IF YOUR BUSINESS'S AXIOM OF QUEST IS MATRIARCH/PATRIARCH:

You get to let go of the reins and stop trying to control your business

You get to understand who your community is, to know and feel why you are the leader of this company

A CHILD WHO SPEAKS THIS LANGUAGE WILL THRIVE IN AN ENVIRONMENT THAT:

Allows them to explore creating and maintaining boundaries

Provides them with ways to feel and accept support

Offers a sense of community

QUESTIONS TO ASK YOUR MATRIARCH/PATRIARCH:

Where am I feeling unsupported and how can I move to feel support?

Where do I feel like I need to control or dictate the situation?

Mentor

Axiom of Quest

Your mission is to guide, tutor, and provide counsel to other individuals on this planet.

You feel happy and purposeful when you are providing guidance to yourself and others. It is important for you to keep in mind that, although you are a guide for others, you are not the final word.

In other words, your mentorships thrive best when you see yourself as a part of an individual's journey. You succeed as a *Mentor* when you are no longer needed. It is also important for you to understand that not everyone *wants* or *needs* a *Mentor*.

INFLUENTIAL WORDS:

Guide

Tutor

Counsel

ABILITIES AND TALENTS:

You have a keen sense of what to say to whom

Your talent is providing insight to individuals to guide them to the next level or phase of their life

CONSCIOUSLY EXPERIENCING THIS LANGUAGE:

Knowing what guidance to provide for yourself

Living without attachment to your mentoring

Incorporating mentorship into your own daily life

Having appropriate mentoring relationships

Choosing your mentorships consciously

UNCONSCIOUSLY EXPERIENCING THIS LANGUAGE:

Losing sight of what you need for yourself

Over-servicing others

Feeling overwhelmed, exhausted, resentful, or angry

Trying to mentor in intimate relationships such that it creates co-dependent relationships

Ignoring your own needs, wants, and desires

Feeling lost and without purpose

SIGNS YOU ARE ON THE PATH:

You have truly supportive teams that can mentor you

You structure your mentorships for balance

You have structure on how to mentor and connect with what you want and desire

You have systems in place for self-care and self-growth

LANGUAGE ORIENTATION:

The *Mentor* is Action/Still. Your Soul has a desire to reflect prior to taking action. If you are under-servicing yourself or over-servicing another, this will place your orientation in more stillness or more action than needed.

ACCESSING AND ATTRACTING SUPPORT:

Caretaker (Axiom of Quest) – This individual's mission is to be "in care" of a belief, theory, or situation. They can help the *Mentor* understand how to mentor their own essence.

Goddess (Axiom of Translation) – These individuals can help the *Mentor* embrace feminine concepts, ideas, and principles in order to accept themselves more fully.

Agent (Tone) – These individuals can help the *Mentor* know when to take action.

IF YOUR BUSINESS'S AXIOM OF QUEST IS MENTOR:

You need to secure formal mentoring with individuals or the company will be undervalued

You need to create appropriate boundaries in the business to prevent over-mentoring

You need to secure mentorships for the business to ensure continued growth

A CHILD WHO SPEAKS THIS LANGUAGE WILL THRIVE IN AN ENVIRONMENT THAT:

Provides the structure for them to create systems of self-care and self-growth

Supports them in recognizing their value

Allows and teaches them to express appropriately what they feel, see, and hear

QUESTIONS TO ASK YOUR MENTOR:

Where do I get to mentor myself?

Where am I over-mentoring? Where do I get to let go and experience something new?

Negotiator

Axiom of Quest

Your mission is all about making a deal and creating new agreements. As a *Negotiator* you sense how compromises can be made to achieve an understanding. Your negotiation relies on strength, will, and an innate knowledge of what needs to happen next.

Influential words:

- Negotiate

- Agreement

- Compromise

Abilities and talents:

You are able to understand what can happen for results and deals to be created

You can see the big picture of interactions and transactions

Consciously experiencing this Language:

Having the foresight to see potential outcomes and know what path each party (including yourself) could take for the best result for all the parties involved

Being unattached to a particular outcome

Knowing that compromise is not a sacrifice

Knowing when a sacred offering—something that you can release, give up or forgo—can be freed for a better deal to be created for yourself and others

Knowing that there are multiple paths to creating each deal

UNCONSCIOUSLY EXPERIENCING THIS LANGUAGE:

Convincing yourself that there is only one particular way to create a deal

Trying to steer the negotiation toward a path that you think is the right direction, instead of allowing others free-will choices

Trying to control the outcome

Being blind to how you are part of a deal

Creating deals that don't sustain you or the life you desire

SIGNS YOU ARE ON THE PATH:

You know what deals you wish to create for yourself

You trust that the deals you are creating serve the highest good, so you have no attachment to the outcomes of the deals

LANGUAGE ORIENTATION:

The *Negotiator* is Action/Still. Your Soul has a desire to reflect prior to moving into action. It is important that you utilize the stillness to really connect with the Divine and see the big picture before moving into the action of creating a deal.

ACCESSING AND ATTRACTING SUPPORT:

Gladiator (Axiom of Quest) – These individuals are champions of a single cause. They can teach the *Negotiator* about championing a cause with compassion and grace.

Gardener (Axiom of Translation) – These individuals are able to nourish and allow things to grow. They can help the *Negotiator* understand what will nourish their own lives and others in order to create deals that allow for growth and expansion.

Beekeeper (Tone) – These individuals are able to communicate effectively, concentrate fully, and work harmoniously in teams. They can help the *Negotiator* to communicate more effectively for more harmonious deals.

IF YOUR BUSINESS'S AXIOM OF QUEST IS NEGOTIATOR:

You are clear about the company's needs and desires for sustainability, and you include them in the deal-making process

Your deals have guidelines: you aren't creating deals for the sake of creating a deal

You attract appropriate partners who are in alignment with the company's mission and purpose

A CHILD WHO SPEAKS THIS LANGUAGE WILL THRIVE IN AN ENVIRONMENT THAT:

Encourages their deal-making abilities

Allows them to see that compromise is not sacrifice

Teaches them to understand their own needs and desires, and how to express them in an appropriate way

QUESTIONS TO ASK YOUR NEGOTIATOR:

What deals or new agreements does my Soul wish to create?

Where am I creating a deal for the sake of creating a deal?

OBSERVER

Axiom of Quest

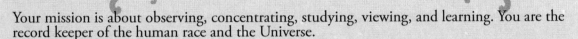

Your mission is about observing, concentrating, studying, viewing, and learning. You are the record keeper of the human race and the Universe.

You can read the Akashic records because, on a metaphysical level, you are a contributor to these records. The Akashic records are knowledge that is held on a non-physical plane of existence. This "library" contains all knowledge of the Universe and human experience.

You are able to witness the signs and "omens" of what you are observing, but may at times feel frustrated that you feel like you do not have the skill to interpret these signs. As an *Observer*, your mission is to witness and view, to state the facts and let others interpret (though an *Observer* may also have other Soul Languages that provide them with the ability to interpret these signs or omens).

INFLUENTIAL WORDS:

Observe

Know

Stillness

ABILITIES AND TALENTS:

You have superhuman powers of observation

You are able to tap into the infinite wisdom of the Universe in order to answer questions

CONSCIOUSLY EXPERIENCING THIS LANGUAGE:

Being able at any time to provide a detailed account of history and information

Understanding that the power of knowledge is within you and not separate from you

Understanding how your observations can help you and others

Being an observing participant

UNCONSCIOUSLY EXPERIENCING THIS LANGUAGE:

Feeling as if your body is limiting

Feeling disconnected from your body

Feeling alone and separate from others

Observing without participating in life

SIGNS YOU ARE ON THE PATH:

You are both observing and participating in life

You are fully in your body

You allow yourself to accept your abilities and be the "seat of perception"

LANGUAGE ORIENTATION:

The *Observer* is Still. Your Soul has a desire for reflection before action. It is important that you understand where movement can be generated or you can get bogged down in the stillness.

ACCESSING AND ATTRACTING SUPPORT:

Negotiator (Axiom of Quest) – These individuals can help the *Observer* create a better deal between their Soul and their body.

Image Maker (Axiom of Translation) – These individuals help bring the Soul into reality. They can help the *Observer* understand what parts of their own Soul they wish to bring forth into reality.

Conductor (Tone) – These individuals understand what brings out the best in others. They can help the *Observer* understand what to highlight inside of them in order to create a better relationship with their own body.

IF YOUR BUSINESS'S AXIOM OF QUEST IS OBSERVER:

You create products and services that are grounded in reality

You communicate clearly about your observations and how they can help others

A CHILD WHO SPEAKS THIS LANGUAGE WILL THRIVE IN AN ENVIRONMENT THAT:

Provides them with an understanding of how to participate in life

Provides them with a strong connection to their body

Provides them with good communication skills

QUESTIONS TO ASK YOUR OBSERVER:

Am I fully grounded in my body?

Where can I participate more in life?

What am I observing and how does it sustain me (or others)?

Peacemaker

Axiom of Quest

Your Soul's mission is to maintain peace for yourself, while also offering peace to individuals and the planet. You can see all sides of a situation and this allows you to bring a totally new perspective to the world and to individuals.

You are a master at resolving conflicts; you neither hide from conflict nor create it.

INFLUENTIAL WORDS:

Stillness

Tranquility

Power

ABILITIES AND TALENTS:

You are able to see all sides of a situation

You can find the "peace center" in yourself and offer that ability to others

You have an innate ability to bring peaceful resolution to a situation

CONSCIOUSLY EXPERIENCING THIS LANGUAGE:

Understanding what you need to feel peaceful

Being able to access the stillness within

Explaining or offering peace to others without judgment or attachment

Knowing what peaceful resolution gets to happen inside of you to achieve your heart's desire

Knowing what peace to offer others for the achievement of their heart's desire

Understanding that your priority is peace

Living in the moment

UNCONSCIOUSLY EXPERIENCING THIS LANGUAGE:

Creating conflict or avoiding it at all costs

Sacrificing your own needs, wants, and desires

Judging yourself or others

Being out of balance with your male and female energies

SIGNS YOU ARE ON THE PATH:

You know where your "peace center" is

You do not sacrifice your peace for others

You are without judgment for yourself and for others

LANGUAGE ORIENTATION:

The *Peacemaker* is Still. Your Soul has a desire to reflect prior to taking action. It is important to be in the stillness to understand which actions will lead to peace.

ACCESSING AND ATTRACTING SUPPORT:

Genius (Axiom of Quest) – This individual's mission is to usher in a new way of thinking that will change history. They can teach the *Peacemaker* how to influence others with support and love.

Emerald (Axiom of Translation) – These individuals are known for their versatility. They can show the *Peacemaker* all the faces of peace.

Closer (Tone) – This individual understands how to bring forth a result. They can help the *Peacemaker* see details on how to create peace that they may have otherwise missed.

Also see the *Guardian* (Tone), page 363.

IF YOUR BUSINESS'S AXIOM OF QUEST IS PEACEMAKER:

You need to instill boundaries for the peace of the business and the people who are part of it

You need to understand what services and/or products you provide that illustrate and provide others with opportunities to be in peace

You need to understand how to operate the business in the present moment

A CHILD WHO SPEAKS THIS LANGUAGE WILL THRIVE IN AN ENVIRONMENT THAT:

Provides them with the ability to live in the moment

Provides them with tools to access their own inner peace

Provides them with the tools to deal with conflict

QUESTIONS TO ASK YOUR PEACEMAKER:

Where am I not allowing peace to be my compass for life's ups and downs?

Where am I not living in the moment?

PIONEER

Axiom of Quest

You have the talent, the desire, and the determination to be the first to open and prepare the way for others. Your mission is to pave the way and create the roads for others to follow in the advancement of this planet.

Thanks to the pioneering efforts of Lewis and Clark, the first settlers of the West were able to develop the infrastructure for towns and cities. In the Christian faith one might describe John the Baptist as a *Pioneer*, in that he provided people with an underlying faith and context which helped prepare them to receive the teachings of Jesus.

INFLUENTIAL WORDS:

Trailblazer

Leader

Adventure

ABILITIES AND TALENTS:

You are able to instantly see where something new can be created

You are able to clear paths of debris so others can travel those roads

CONSCIOUSLY EXPERIENCING THIS LANGUAGE:

Understanding what seeds to spread over the land for others to further expand

Knowing what seeds to sow for your own Soul

Creating new pathways that are in alignment with body, mind, and spirit

Forging new paths without attachment

Attracting others who support your spirit

Feeling supported and having community

UNCONSCIOUSLY EXPERIENCING THIS LANGUAGE:

Being unable to see the road that needs paving

Trying to pave a road that doesn't need paving

Creating distractions by paving too many new roads

Feeling alienated, thinking people just don't "get" you

Feeling like you are doing it alone

SIGNS YOU ARE ON THE PATH:

You know what new road you wish to travel and create

You have a supportive community around you

You know what seeds to sow for yourself

LANGUAGE ORIENTATION:

The *Pioneer* is Action. Your Soul has a desire to move directly into action. It is important for the *Pioneer* to really determine if the action they are taking is in alignment with body, mind, and spirit to avoid forging new roads as a distraction.

ACCESSING AND ATTRACTING SUPPORT:

Mentor (Axiom of Quest) – These individuals can provide insight on what guidance the *Pioneer* needs to pave their own roads.

Image Maker (Axiom of Translation) – These individuals can help the *Pioneer* understand what their Soul wishes to bring into reality. This will help the *Pioneer* see new roads for themselves and others.

Sovereign (Tone) – These individuals have an understanding of and desire to express their power. They know that they are able to create their own lives. They can help the *Pioneer* accept and understand their own power.

IF YOUR BUSINESS'S AXIOM OF QUEST IS PIONEER:

You need to understand what new road(s) you are paving

You need to be confident in the abilities of the company without being attached to everyone being able to "get" what the company is accomplishing

You need to be focused in your creating

A CHILD WHO SPEAKS THIS LANGUAGE WILL THRIVE IN AN ENVIRONMENT THAT:

Provides them with opportunities to explore what they wish to create

Provides them with the knowledge that they are breaking new ground

Provides them with an understanding of how to attract and recognize their community

QUESTIONS TO ASK YOUR PIONEER:

What road do I keep trying to forge that is a distraction?

What new path would I like to create for myself?

Where do I need to feel support in order to recognize that I'm not alone?

POLITICIAN

Axiom of Quest

Your mission is to be involved with and influence the way humans feel, govern, think about and express themselves.

In many ways, you are here to "govern" the structure of humanity. You are able to provide yourself and others the forum to speak, feel, and express their beliefs and ideas. You can help create for yourself and others the space or forum to feel and speak the truth of the Soul.

INFLUENTIAL WORDS:

Space

Truth

Speak

ABILITIES AND TALENTS:

You are able to create a safe space for the expression of truth

You are able to know when the truth (material from Source) is being spoken

CONSCIOUSLY EXPERIENCING THIS LANGUAGE:

Governing with the focus of love, harmony, and balance, and with the intention of the greatest good of all

Being aware of your truth and giving yourself the forum to express it

Creating the forum for others to express their truth

Unconsciously experiencing this Language:

Lacking boundaries or providing the space for others to speak their truth in an inappropriate way towards you

Trying to choose what another's truth is

Forcing your beliefs and truths on others

Ignoring your own truth

Avoiding hearing or expressing your own truth

Signs you are on the path:

You know your truth and express it appropriately

You set appropriate boundaries

You allow yourself time for connection to understand your truth on a deeper level

Language Orientation:

The *Politician* is Action/Still. Your Soul has a desire for solitude or reflection prior to committing to action. It is in this quiet that you will discover and explore your truth in order to understand what the next Divinely inspired action could be.

Accessing and Attracting Support:

Caretaker (Axiom of Quest) – These individuals are the custodians of a belief, theory, person or object. They can show the *Politician* how to care with proper boundaries.

Messenger (Axiom of Translation) – This individual can help the *Politician* learn to hear the different messages of "truth".

Bodybuilder (Tone) – These individuals are able to build up form and Soul. They can teach the *Politician* how to perceive the building blocks of form and Soul in order to understand how form and Soul fit together and see where truth can be built up.

If your business's Axiom of Quest is Politician:

You create appropriate boundaries for feedback

You explore the "truth" of the business

You structure the expression of the truth of the business

A child who speaks this Language will thrive in an environment that:

Provides them with an understanding that it is safe to appropriately express their truth

Provides them with an understanding that their truth is not everyone's truth

Provides them with healthy boundaries for service and love

Questions to ask your Politician:

What is my truth?

What space do I get to give myself to hear or express my truth?

In what medium would I like to express my truth?

Prophet

Axiom of Quest

Your mission is to generate change for the planet, the world, and the Universe by delivering and distributing the message(s) of Divine inspiration.

A perfect example of the *Prophet* is Noah. Noah was given a message with a plan and a structure to save the world from the great flood.

Influential words:

Message

Structure

Visionary

Abilities and Talents:

You are able to "see" or predict from Divine inspiration what is to come

You have the gift of inspiration

Consciously experiencing this Language:

Hearing and understanding the message(s)

Understanding the structure that will allow the message to take form so that humans can be helped

Understanding that you don't need to know every step of the plan in advance, just one step at a time

Feeling connected to the Divine and expressing Divine voice

UNCONSCIOUSLY EXPERIENCING THIS LANGUAGE:

Being unable to hear your own message

Feeling afraid to express Divine voice

Feeling weighed down by having to know every part of the plan or structure

Feeling paralyzed, especially by the fear of being responsible for what others do with the message

SIGNS YOU ARE ON THE PATH:

You understand and hear your own Divine message

You are speaking your truth

LANGUAGE ORIENTATION:

The *Prophet* is Action/Still. Your Soul has a desire to reflect prior to creating. It is important that you utilize the stillness to hear and interpret the message(s).

ACCESSING AND ATTRACTING SUPPORT:

Genius (Axiom of Quest) – These individuals help usher the world into a new way of existence. They can help add structure to a message for a *Prophet*.

Nurturer (Axiom of Translation) – These individuals can provide balance. They can help the *Prophet* nurture themselves with respect to their own message.

Deliberator (Tone) – These individuals are the great decision-makers. They can help the *Prophet* feel safe to express their message(s).

Also see the *Guardian* (Tone), page 363.

IF YOUR BUSINESS'S AXIOM OF QUEST IS PROPHET:

The company message is clear

The company has a clear structure to deliver its message(s)

The company has clear policies and expectations

A CHILD WHO SPEAKS THIS LANGUAGE WILL THRIVE IN AN ENVIRONMENT THAT:

Allows them to feel safe speaking the truth

Provides them with the understanding that they don't need to know every part of a plan or structure

Provides them with a balance of still and action

QUESTIONS TO ASK YOUR PROPHET:

Where am I not hearing Divine messages? What do I get to let go of in order to hear them?

Where can I utilize my Divine voice more?

Significator

Axiom of Quest

Your mission is to guide people in understanding, to point them on the path to their own individual mission.

You are able to awaken individuals to their own consciousness and journey.

Influential words:

Path

Mission

Purpose

Abilities and Talents:

You are able to provide opportunities for others to blossom and grow

You are able to see and understand individual paths

Consciously experiencing this Language:

Being able to feel, see, and know what journey or consciousness gets to be awakened in you

Providing opportunities for others to activate their own journey, with grace and without attachment

Experiencing the consciousness of love and pure intention for yourself and others

Walking your talk

UNCONSCIOUSLY EXPERIENCING THIS LANGUAGE:

Being stuck in your greatest challenge

Manipulating others for your own personal gain

Feeling overcome with fear and doubt

Being unable to see your own path

SIGNS YOU ARE ON THE PATH:

You know your own path

You are living on purpose

You understand your greatest challenge

LANGUAGE ORIENTATION:

The *Significator* is Action. Your Soul has a desire to move into action quickly. It is important that you set up structure for reflection so you can act on Divine guidance.

ACCESSING AND ATTRACTING SUPPORT:

Politician (Axiom of Quest) – These individuals provide a forum for others to speak their truth. They can help the *Significator* understand that everyone has their own truth.

Image Maker (Axiom of Translation) – These individuals are able to see a Soul's potential and bring it into reality. They can help the *Significator* understand what part of their own Soul's potential they wish to bring forth into reality.

Conductor (Tone) – These individuals understand what to highlight in individuals that will bring out the best in them. They can help the *Significator* to bring out their own best.

IF YOUR BUSINESS'S AXIOM OF QUEST IS SIGNIFICATOR:

You are clear about the mission of the company

You are clear about what you are offering

Your marketing is not based on fear

A CHILD WHO SPEAKS THIS LANGUAGE WILL THRIVE IN AN ENVIRONMENT THAT:

Provides them with tools to understand the free-will choices of others

Provides them with a foundation for self-love and respect

Provides them with a foundation of ethics and morals

QUESTIONS TO ASK YOUR SIGNIFICATOR:

What am I activating within myself?

What do I need to understand in order for my path to be more visible?

CHAPTER 6:

Axiom of Translation – Fueling Your Mission

You will learn in this chapter:

- The different Axioms of Translation

- How to collaborate with your Axiom of Translation

- Questions for your Axiom of Translation

Axiom of Translation

Your Axiom of Translation reveals two aspects of your Soul. First, it describes how you will be known here on this planet. Think of the words other people use to describe you. These often correspond to your Axiom of Translation. For example, if your Axiom of Translation is *Nurturer* you might find that others describe you as giving, loving, nurturing, etc.

The Axiom of Translation also describes what tools and talents you use to fuel your mission. For example, if your Axiom of Quest is *Pioneer* and your Axiom of Translation is *Heart Conscious*, you will be fueling your mission of forging new roads (*Pioneer*) by opening up your heart and others' hearts to love (*Heart Conscious*).

Collaborating with Your Axiom of Translation

Understanding and bringing consciousness to this Language allows you to:

- Be Divinely guided in the "how" of things

- Let go of limiting beliefs that are preventing you from moving forward and experiencing life without struggle

- Understand and accept your talents in a deeper way

- Receive more guidance about the next steps on your journey

Intention Setting

Create a conscious connection with your Axiom of Translation and complete the sentence below:

My personal intention for how I utilize my gifts and talents today is...

Want to add additional power to your intention? Write it down in your journal and say it out loud.

Questions for Your Axiom of Translation

Create a conscious connection with your Axiom of Translation. Then ask these questions to initiate a conversation:

What do I get to accept, allow, activate or let go of today that will allow me to utilize more of my Soulful resources?

What action can I take today that will allow me to utilize those resources for the greatest good?

Where in my life am I handing over my power?

What do I get to accept, allow, activate or let go of in order to fully express my power?

What are some triggers that move me from consciously expressing this Language to unconsciously expressing this Language?

How can I co-create with this part of my Soul to create a more powerful life?

For additional questions, see the definition of your Axiom of Translation.

Axiom of Translation Language Definitions

There are 33 Languages in this category. As you understand your Axiom of Translation more fully, you will receive more guidance to interpret the individual steps and experiences of your Soul's agenda.

APPRENTICE

Axiom of Translation

You will be known here for how you observe and translate what you learn into tangible skills or creations. You have an appreciation for details and the "nuts and bolts" of how things work. Your attention to detail and precise manner allow you to become a master craftsman.

INFLUENTIAL WORDS:

Talents

Observe

Create

ABILITIES AND TALENTS:

You are able to turn an observation into a tangible skill

You are able to apply skills in a variety of contexts

CONSCIOUSLY EXPERIENCING THIS LANGUAGE:

Understanding how processes can be used to benefit different areas of your life

Understanding how small details fit into the big picture

Focusing in alignment with your life purpose

Knowing what skills and talents you bring to situations

UNCONSCIOUSLY EXPERIENCING THIS LANGUAGE:

Keeping yourself busy as a form of distraction or a way of hiding out

Just observing and not creating

Judging your skills and talents

Getting lost in the details

SIGNS YOU ARE ON THE PATH:

You are aware of what skills and talents you are bringing to a situation

You are aware of the big picture and how the details fit into that picture

LANGUAGE ORIENTATION:

The *Apprentice* is Action/Still. Your Soul has a desire to reflect prior to taking action. This will allow you to observe and then turn those observations into skills or create something new.

ACCESSING AND ATTRACTING SUPPORT:

Politician (Axiom of Quest) – These individuals help provide a forum to speak the truth. They can help the *Apprentice* share their observations without fear.

Lawmaker (Axiom of Translation) – These individuals help create structure for peace. They can help the *Apprentice* create structure to feel safe being who they are.

Diplomat (Tone) – These individuals help others create new deals out of love. They can help the *Apprentice* let go of self-judgment.

IF YOUR BUSINESS'S AXIOM OF TRANSLATION IS APPRENTICE:

You are clear what observations and skills you are offering

You continually update your business systems

You promote the fact that the company is detail-oriented

A CHILD WHO SPEAKS THIS LANGUAGE WILL THRIVE IN AN ENVIRONMENT THAT:

Provides them with a structure to support and nurture their skill for detail in a healthy manner

Provides them with the appropriate channels for self-expression

Provides them with a variety of ways to create

QUESTIONS TO ASK YOUR APPRENTICE:

What do I wish to create?

What observation can I turn into a skill?

CATALYST

Axiom of Translation

You will be known here as an agent of change. Your energy can provide and/or precipitate an event, situation, or action that creates transformation without you being consumed or affected.

You prefer not to offer these moments of change until a conclusion or transformation is available. Your energy can provide a more Divinely guided route, which allows those involved in that event or situation to transform with less struggle and more power.

INFLUENTIAL WORDS:

Transform

Momentum

Influence

ABILITIES AND TALENTS:

You are able to "speed up" transformation and not be consumed by the process

You provide others with the opportunity to experience their power more gracefully

CONSCIOUSLY EXPERIENCING THIS LANGUAGE:

Understanding how to be your own agent of change

Offering opportunities to others that are in the greatest good of all

Knowing that regeneration occurs in your relationship with the Divine

Living in the present, where miracles happen and transformation takes place

Promoting change and transformation without attachment

Feeling renewed by being of true service to yourself and others

Following your innate knowing of when a situation is complete

UNCONSCIOUSLY EXPERIENCING THIS LANGUAGE:

Feeling drained because of your attachment to the change that you offer others

Repeatedly offering change to others because you are attached to a certain outcome or conclusion

Experiencing constant doubt, fear, and judgment

Feeling responsible for others' emotions, decisions, and choices

Creating co-dependent relationships

SIGNS YOU ARE ON THE PATH:

You have a spiritual practice in place for your personal regeneration

You allow for your own change and transformation

You are creating healthy and supportive relationships

LANGUAGE ORIENTATION:

The *Catalyst* is Action. Your Soul has a desire to move directly into action. It is important that you utilize your connection with the Divine to create inspired action and not action just for the sake of action.

ACCESSING AND ATTRACTING SUPPORT:

Mentor (Axiom of Quest) – These individuals can support the *Catalyst* by providing them with skills to guide rather than push others to an opportunity for change.

Motivator (Axiom of Translation) – These individuals can help the *Catalyst* determine their true motivation for offering others opportunities for change.

Diplomat (Tone) – These individuals help others create new deals out of love. They can help the *Catalyst* let go of self-judgment and criticism.

IF YOUR BUSINESS'S AXIOM OF TRANSLATION IS CATALYST:

You are clear what kinds of transformation you offer

You have structures in place for appropriate client feedback

You set aside time for regeneration, for both the company and its employees

A CHILD WHO SPEAKS THIS LANGUAGE WILL THRIVE IN AN ENVIRONMENT THAT:

Provides them with a structure for faith and connection to the Divine

Provides them with models of healthy relationships

Provides them with a balanced model of self-love and self-growth

QUESTIONS TO ASK YOUR CATALYST:

Where am I attached in this situation?

How can I be more present in this situation?

Constable

Axiom of Translation

You will be known here for having the power to help yourself and others maintain peace.

Influential words:

Harmony

Sustainability

Order

Abilities and talents:

You are able to offer the opportunity for sustainable peace for yourself and others

You are a "born leader" and wise

Consciously experiencing this Language:

Understanding and keeping the peace within yourself

Resonating leadership and a calming authority

Having a clear definition of what peace means to you

Being respectful of others' free-will decisions

Not being attached to maintaining the peace you are offering others

UNCONSCIOUSLY EXPERIENCING THIS LANGUAGE:

Placing yourself in authority of situations, events, or people that have not given you permission or requested your involvement

Being unable to find and maintain your peace

Being attached to what you are offering others

Judging yourself and others

Trying to maintain peace by forced control

SIGNS YOU ARE ON THE PATH:

You have a clear definition of peace for yourself

You are in unconditional love for yourself

You are respectful of other people's free-will choices and offer peace without attachment

LANGUAGE ORIENTATION:

The *Constable* is Action/Still. Your Soul has a desire to reflect prior to taking action. This will allow you to maintain your own peace while offering others the opportunity to find their own.

ACCESSING AND ATTRACTING SUPPORT:

Pioneer (Axiom of Quest) – These individuals help forge new roads for others. They can help the *Constable* understand new avenues of peace for themselves and other individuals.

Motivator (Axiom of Translation) – These individuals help to spring people into action. They can help show the *Constable* what the motivation is for maintaining peace and what their motivation would be for allowing chaos.

Conductor (Tone) – These individuals can help the *Constable* learn to see the best in individuals so peace can be achieved with ease and grace.

Also see the *Guardian* (Tone), page 363.

IF YOUR BUSINESS'S AXIOM OF TRANSLATION IS CONSTABLE:

You are clear what type of peace you are offering your clients

You are without attachment to your offerings, knowing that you are at peace and provided for no matter what

You are clear in marketing materials and mission statements about the leadership role of your company

A CHILD WHO SPEAKS THIS LANGUAGE WILL THRIVE IN AN ENVIRONMENT THAT:

Provides them with tools to create and maintain peace in their life

Provides them with tools to be a compassionate and wise leader

Models respect for other people's choices

QUESTIONS TO ASK YOUR CONSTABLE:

Where am I trying to maintain peace through force or control?

What does peace mean to me in this situation?

CREATOR

Axiom of Translation

You will be known here for your ability to breathe into existence something that has never been in existence before.

INFLUENTIAL WORDS:

Original

Creative

Innovative

ABILITIES AND TALENTS:

You are able to shed new light on things so something can be seen that hasn't been seen before

You are innately able to bring things into existence via the process of inspiration

CONSCIOUSLY EXPERIENCING THIS LANGUAGE:

Allowing the power of creation to flow through you

Allowing for the process of creation

Understanding where you want to focus your creative powers

Being true to yourself

Offering your creative talents and gifts to others, knowing that you are loved, supported, and provided for by Universal flow

Knowing your "place" in life

UNCONSCIOUSLY EXPERIENCING THIS LANGUAGE:

Feeling stuck

Listening to the "inner critic"

Believing that you lack creative power

Feeling as if you don't belong

Hiding out

Trying to control the creative process

SIGNS YOU ARE ON THE PATH:

You accept that you have a different way of doing things

You allow the creative process to flow with Divine timing

LANGUAGE ORIENTATION:

The *Creator* is Action/Still. Your Soul has a desire to reflect prior to taking action. It is important that you allow yourself time for reflection in order to truly understand what action will support your creative process.

ACCESSING AND ATTRACTING SUPPORT:

Mentor (Axiom of Quest) – These individuals can help mentor the *Creator* in listening to their own guidance. This will help them determine what their *Creator* wishes to create.

Motivator (Axiom of Translation) – These individuals can help the *Creator* determine what their motivation in life is, either fear or love.

Evolver (Tone) – These individuals prefer to go through life constantly evolving and transforming. They can help the *Creator* understand their next evolutionary path.

IF YOUR BUSINESS'S AXIOM OF TRANSLATION IS CREATOR:

You need to focus the energy of the business so it isn't spread too thin

You need to provide a channel for client feedback that allows the company to correct its course and draw creativity from knowledge instead of fear

You need to understand the company's "place" in its industry

A CHILD WHO SPEAKS THIS LANGUAGE WILL THRIVE IN AN ENVIRONMENT THAT:

Provides them with an outlet for their creative energy

Provides them with a sense of community that allows them to feel safe and supported

Provides them with opportunities to explore their creative genius

QUESTIONS TO ASK YOUR CREATOR:

What do I wish to create?

Where am I afraid of being myself or of what other people will think?

Emerald

Axiom of Translation

You will be known here for your many sides, your versatility, and your multi-faceted nature. You might even be referred to as a Renaissance man or woman.

Emeralds as gems are not as "strong" as diamonds, so most emeralds are treated in order to protect them. Their clarity is graded by the visible eye. An emerald is considered flawless when it doesn't have any visible inclusions or surface-breaking fissures. Flawless emeralds are rare. Inclusions are tolerated, and fine emeralds can be even more valuable than diamonds.

INFLUENTIAL WORDS:

> Versatility
>
> Brilliance
>
> Journey

ABILITIES AND TALENTS:

> You are able to see the many sides of a situation, a person, etc.
>
> You have many talents, sides, and faces

CONSCIOUSLY EXPERIENCING THIS LANGUAGE:

> Feeling flawless inside, meaning you feel at one with the Universe and the Divine
>
> Understanding your Divinity and helping others to understand theirs
>
> Balancing your versatility with focus
>
> Knowing that everyone has the ability to be priceless
>
> Knowing that the purpose is not the destination, but rather it is the journey
>
> Revealing your brilliance to yourself and the world
>
> Creating healthy multi-faceted relationships

UNCONSCIOUSLY EXPERIENCING THIS LANGUAGE:

Feeling trapped and unable to move

Seeing only the flaws in yourself and others

Focusing too much on the destination

Hiding out

Being one-sided in nature

Creating relationships that are not fulfilling

SIGNS YOU ARE ON THE PATH:

You are always polishing yourself by learning new skills and educating yourself

You are in unconditional love with yourself

You are not hiding out by searching for new talents

LANGUAGE ORIENTATION:

The *Emerald* is Action/Still. Your Soul has a desire to reflect before taking action. This will allow you to see all sides of a situation, determine which of your talents are relevant, and then take action.

ACCESSING AND ATTRACTING SUPPORT:

Matriarch/Patriarch (Axiom of Quest) – The purpose of the *Matriarch/Patriarch* is to lead. They can help the *Emerald* feel safe and supported.

Huntress/Hunter (Axiom of Translation) – These individuals help others to hunt or gather what they desire or need. They can help the *Emerald* be focused in their pursuits.

Collaborator (Tone) – These individuals are co-creative by nature. They can help the *Emerald* create relationships that are based on support and not just one-sided.

IF YOUR BUSINESS'S AXIOM OF TRANSLATION IS EMERALD:

You need to clearly communicate all of the company's talents

You need to have a clear system in place for attracting new talent to the company

You have strategies and systems in place to maintain focus

A CHILD WHO SPEAKS THIS LANGUAGE WILL THRIVE IN AN ENVIRONMENT THAT:

Provides them with a variety of different learning experiences

Provides them with appropriate ways to express their feelings and ideas

Provides them with experiences that support the idea that "there is more than one side" to a situation

QUESTIONS TO ASK YOUR EMERALD:

What skill or talent do I have that can help or nurture this situation?

How can I enjoy my journey more fully?

Gardener

Axiom of Translation

You will be known here as a master "planter" and "cultivator". You listen to, provide for, and nourish anything and everything so it can grow. You can help others to break up the soil of their lives so new "things" can take root and grow.

Influential words:

Develop

Cultivate

Grow

Abilities and Talents:

You are able to nourish anything to grow

You are able to teach others how to plant seeds that will bear fruit

Consciously experiencing this Language:

Understanding what nutrients you need for your own life to grow

Understanding what you are planting in your own life

Understanding how to co-create with the Universe so growth can happen gracefully

Understanding what beliefs, thoughts, and ideas are rooted in your own life that may be preventing new things from growing

Understanding what to focus on so it grows

UNCONSCIOUSLY EXPERIENCING THIS LANGUAGE:

Trying to control how something grows, what it grows, or where it grows

Losing interest or faith before something has the chance to blossom

Feeling unsupported

Being unaware of what your life needs, wants, or desires in order to grow

Over-servicing others

Focusing on fear and doubt

SIGNS YOU ARE ON THE PATH:

You know what you wish to create in your own life

You are providing or receiving resources to nurture your life to grow

LANGUAGE ORIENTATION:

The *Gardener* is Action/Still. Your Soul has a desire to reflect prior to moving into action. This reflection or stillness will allow you to be a better partner with the Universe.

ACCESSING AND ATTRACTING SUPPORT:

Prophet (Axiom of Quest) – These individuals can help *Gardeners* understand the "message" of their lives and how to create the structure that supports this message.

Nurturer (Axiom of Translation) – These individuals can help *Gardeners* understand ways to support and nurture their lives.

Diplomat (Tone) – These individuals help others create new deals through love. They can help the *Gardener* understand what tools (fear, love, etc.) they are using to create their relationships.

IF YOUR BUSINESS'S AXIOM OF TRANSLATION IS GARDENER:

You understand what the company needs to focus its energy on to "grow"

You are creating sustainable, nurturing joint ventures

You allow for appropriate development and growth of ideas, products, services, programs, etc.

A CHILD WHO SPEAKS THIS LANGUAGE WILL THRIVE IN AN ENVIRONMENT THAT:

Provides them with a strong sense of trust and faith

Provides them with examples and models of co-creative relationships

Provides them with structures for healthy self-care and self-awareness

QUESTIONS TO ASK YOUR GARDENER:

Where am I trying to control a situation that is preventing growth for me?

Where can I use more nourishment in my life?

GODDESS

Axiom of Translation

You will be known here for your feminine concepts, ideas, principles, attributes, and energy. You can do this via traditional feminine concepts or by creating new concepts and beliefs.

This Language is not about being a particular gender, but rather about the energy you embody.

INFLUENTIAL WORDS:

Energy

Power

Receiving

ABILITIES AND TALENTS:

You are able to bask in the splendor of being feminine

You can see how others create unnecessary structure that is non-beneficial and outdated

CONSCIOUSLY EXPERIENCING THIS LANGUAGE:

Knowing and accepting your own definition of femininity

Being at home with your own femininity

Expressing this energy to the world

Accepting the feminine power within you

Being balanced in giving and receiving

Creating sacred time for stillness and listening and then moving into action

UNCONSCIOUSLY EXPERIENCING THIS LANGUAGE:

Being in a battle with your feminine or masculine side

Being unbalanced with your feminine and masculine energy

Not recognizing and accepting the *Goddess* within you

Expressing your feminine nature according to what you *think* it is supposed to be

Focusing only on giving and not receiving, or on receiving and not giving

SIGNS YOU ARE ON THE PATH:

You have your own definition of femininity

You are balanced in your masculine and feminine energies

LANGUAGE ORIENTATION:

The *Goddess* is Still. Your Soul has a desire to reflect. It is important that you allow that reflection time to feel your power within.

ACCESSING AND ATTRACTING SUPPORT:

Pioneer (Axiom of Quest) – These individuals help themselves and others forge new roads. They can help the *Goddess* create their own path.

Motivator (Axiom of Translation) – These individuals can help the *Goddess* understand their motivation in creating their own life.

Connoisseur (Tone) – These individuals are all about acceptance. They can help the *Goddess* accept all parts of themselves.

IF YOUR BUSINESS'S AXIOM OF TRANSLATION IS GODDESS:

You are clear about what you are offering and provide avenues for receiving

You allow the company to express its power

You create time for reflection

A CHILD WHO SPEAKS THIS LANGUAGE WILL THRIVE IN AN ENVIRONMENT THAT:

Provides them with an acceptance of their feminine energy

Provides them with appropriate feminine role models

Provides them with the ability to both give and receive

QUESTIONS TO ASK YOUR GODDESS:

Where am I not allowing for the possibilities of the Universe?

Where can I open up to receiving more?

Heart Conscious

Axiom of Translation

You will be known here as one who experiences the world through the heart and its expression – love.

This love is not based on the mind. It is a state of being which is unconditional, fixed, and everlasting.

Influential words:

One

Emotion

Unconditional

Abilities and Talents:

You have the power to see that everyone is whole and complete

You have an unlimited source of unconditional love to offer yourself and others

Consciously experiencing this Language:

Understanding that love is not reliant on external forces

Understanding that unconditional love can move mountains in your world and in the world of others

Understanding that you are whole and choosing not to separate yourself from this truth

Creating true supportive relationships with like-minded individuals

Understanding and feeling that we are all one

Allowing the mind to follow the heart

UNCONSCIOUSLY EXPERIENCING THIS LANGUAGE:

Having a hard time expressing your emotions; this may show up as depression, denying your feelings, or reacting explosively

People-pleasing or creating co-dependent relationships

Creating situations that give you the perception that you are separate from the Divine, the Universe, or humanity

Using love in its conditional forms (e.g. possessiveness, addiction, control)

SIGNS YOU ARE ON THE PATH:

You are loving to yourself

You have created unconditional, co-creative relationships

You express your emotions appropriately

LANGUAGE ORIENTATION:

The *Heart Conscious* is Still. Your Soul has a desire for reflection. In this stillness you can experience the consciousness of love.

ACCESSING AND ATTRACTING SUPPORT:

Observer (Axiom of Quest) – These individuals have access to all knowing. They can help the *Heart Conscious* individual observe the facts.

Image Maker (Axiom of Translation) – These individuals see the Soul and help bring that into reality. They can help the *Heart Conscious* individual understand action, as opposed to Soul.

Captain (Tone) – These individuals can help the *Heart Conscious* individual develop structures for expressing love for themselves.

IF YOUR BUSINESS'S AXIOM OF TRANSLATION IS HEART CONSCIOUS:

You understand that the company is providing wholeness to its customers

You have clear boundaries in place to create beneficial and nurturing relationships for the business

You understand that it is hard for some individuals to be in the presence of unconditional love

A CHILD WHO SPEAKS THIS LANGUAGE WILL THRIVE IN AN ENVIRONMENT THAT:

Supports them being friends with different groups of people

Provides them with a strong sense of self in order to say "No!" when it is in their best interest

Provides them with ways to nurture and show themselves love

QUESTIONS TO ASK YOUR HEART CONSCIOUS:

What emotions am I not expressing?

Why am I feeling separate from the Divine?

Herald

Axiom of Translation

You will be known here as a forerunner. You bring news, information, and announcements; you can indicate or signal that change is coming.

Your news helps and guides you and others into change and transformation.

Influential words:

Forerunner

Signs

Change

Abilities and talents:

You are able to signal that a new movement is coming

You are able to see way ahead of your time

Consciously experiencing this Language:

Being aware of the signs of change

Being free of attachment to what others might say about the news you are bringing forth

Knowing that you are speaking the truth

Feeling loved and supported

Allowing for a clear, conscious connection with the Universe without fear and judgment

Having a clear platform to distribute the "news"

UNCONSCIOUSLY EXPERIENCING THIS LANGUAGE:

Seeking outside validation

Fearing and/or doubting that the news you are bringing is accurate

Conducting your life by jury

Comparing yourself to others

Distributing ego-based "news"

Fearing change

SIGNS YOU ARE ON THE PATH:

You have a clear platform to distribute your "news"

You are aware of and expressing your truth

You are unafraid of the signs and changes you are witnessing

LANGUAGE ORIENTATION:

The *Herald* is Action/Still. Your Soul has a desire to move into action after reflection. This will allow you to understand as fully as you can the messages, news, and signs of change.

ACCESSING AND ATTRACTING SUPPORT:

Negotiator (Axiom of Quest) – These individuals help others create better deals for themselves. They can help the *Herald* to create win-win situations.

Partner (Axiom of Translation) – These individuals help others establish co-creative partnerships. They can help the *Herald* create authentic support teams.

Connoisseur (Tone) – These individuals are all about acceptance. They can help the *Herald* love and accept themselves.

IF YOUR BUSINESS'S AXIOM OF TRANSLATION IS HERALD:

You are clear about the opportunities for change you are offering people

You have a clear platform to distribute the information of change

You have a team in place to allow for some transitions during change

A CHILD WHO SPEAKS THIS LANGUAGE WILL THRIVE IN AN ENVIRONMENT THAT:

Provides them with appropriate ways to express themselves

Provides them with a structure to support their ability to see way beyond what others see

Provides them with a structure that allows them to feel loved, supported, and provided for

QUESTIONS TO ASK YOUR HERALD:

Where am I feeling attachment in this situation, and why?

What structure or platform could I use to distribute this information?

HERO

Axiom of Translation

You will be known here for your innate ability to complete a task that might seem overwhelming and inconceivable to others.

Often the *Hero* will have an inner calling that there is something bigger out in the world to experience, and will answer this call from within.

INFLUENTIAL WORDS:

Action

Possibilities

Inconceivable

ABILITIES AND TALENTS:

You are able to take action when others are afraid to move

You have gifts and talents that you offer to others to improve the world around you

CONSCIOUSLY EXPERIENCING THIS LANGUAGE:

Answering the call within you

Allowing the support of the Divine and others to help you on your journey

Seeing the possibilities and knowing that the world is unlimited

Trusting the journey

UNCONSCIOUSLY EXPERIENCING THIS LANGUAGE:

Hearing the Divine call to action but being afraid to answer it

Feeling not good enough

Feeling disconnected from your higher power

Feeling overwhelmed

Attracting situations or challenges to prove your worth

SIGNS YOU ARE ON THE PATH:

You understand the steps in your journey and face them with courage

You are clear about your gifts and talents

You allow yourself to receive support from the Universe

LANGUAGE ORIENTATION:

The *Hero* is Action. Your Soul has a desire to move directly into action. It is important that you allow for Divine inspiration prior to taking action. This will allow you to receive the resources needed for your journey.

ACCESSING AND ATTRACTING SUPPORT:

Mentor (Axiom of Quest) – These individuals provide guidance and support. They can help the *Hero* mentor their talents and gifts.

Problem Solver (Axiom of Translation) – These individuals help to see a solution immediately. They can help the *Hero* see solutions to challenges on their journey.

Diplomat (Tone) – These individuals help others create new relationships. They can help the *Hero* create supportive, loving relationships.

IF YOUR BUSINESS'S AXIOM OF TRANSLATION IS HERO:

You need to understand what journey you are offering to others

You need to know what talents and gifts you are offering to others

You have systems in place to avoid feeling overwhelmed

A CHILD WHO SPEAKS THIS LANGUAGE WILL THRIVE IN AN ENVIRONMENT THAT:

Provides them with an understanding of their gifts and talents

Provides them with a connection to their higher power

Supports them in their belief that anything is possible

QUESTIONS TO ASK YOUR HERO:

What am I afraid of that is preventing me from moving forward in my journey?

What talents and gifts am I offering to others?

Huntress/Hunter

Axiom of Translation

You will be known here for how you engage, explore, track, and secure what you are seeking.

You are able to determine and understand the direction or path something will take. The *Huntress* (female energy) or *Hunter* (male energy) can understand their target by tracking (male energy), gathering (female energy), exploring (male and female energy), or by having an inner knowing (male and female energy).

Influential words:

Gather

Seek

Understand

Abilities and talents:

You know where to look for what is needed

You have a keen sense of exploration, of finding and securing

Consciously experiencing this Language:

Being in harmony with the thing you are seeking

Knowing when to hunt (insistently pursue) and when to simply gather (pause and receive)

Being balanced in your feminine and masculine energies

Unconsciously experiencing this Language:

Hunting (or seeking) for sport, without Divine inspiration

Not knowing what you are pursuing or want to pursue

Not receiving what you desire

Not feeling safe being vulnerable

Signs you are on the path:

You have a clear understanding of what your inspired actions are

You know when to gather and when to hunt

You are balanced in your female and male energies

Language Orientation:

The *Huntress/Hunter* is Action. Your Soul has a desire to take action. If you don't take time to listen to Divine inspiration, you may be taking action for action's sake. This will result in pursuing without receiving.

Accessing and Attracting Support:

Avatar (Axiom of Quest) – The *Avatar's* mission is to be an embodiment of a belief or principle. They can support the *Huntress/Hunter* in receiving love and compassion.

Messenger (Axiom of Translation) – This individual can help the *Huntress/Hunter* learn to hear the different messages of what they are truly seeking.

Conductor (Tone) – These individuals can help the *Huntress/Hunter* learn to see the best in individuals so they can become comfortable with vulnerability.

IF YOUR BUSINESS'S AXIOM OF TRANSLATION IS HUNTRESS/HUNTER:

You need a balance between action and creation

You need to know what you are seeking

You need to know your goal or intended result

A CHILD WHO SPEAKS THIS LANGUAGE WILL THRIVE IN AN ENVIRONMENT THAT:

Allows them to see different approaches to giving and receiving

Provides them with balanced beliefs about male and female energy

Supports them in feeling safe being vulnerable

QUESTIONS TO ASK YOUR HUNTRESS/HUNTER:

Where do I need to receive?

Where am I trying to hunt instead of gather?

IMAGE MAKER

Axiom of Translation

You will be known for having the ability to picture the essence of something and then share that image with others to help bring it forth into reality.

You are able to see the Soul of a person, and to bring that Soul's fullest expression forth into reality.

For example, you can see the Hollywood star in the face of the farm girl and then help unveil and reveal that image for others. Or, like Michelangelo, you can see the sculpture within a solid piece of marble.

The *Image Maker* has the ability to see the image of the Divine in humans, and to bring that image into reality.

INFLUENTIAL WORDS:

Soul

Essence

Reality

ABILITIES AND TALENTS:

You are able to see the essence of a human and how to bring that forth

You see past the fluff and the façade to the core of what is real

CONSCIOUSLY EXPERIENCING THIS LANGUAGE:

Knowing that identity and persona are not the true essence of an individual

Knowing what parts or images of your Soul you want to bring forth into your reality

Presenting ideas, thoughts, and images in a non-judgmental and loving way

Creating balanced relationships with individuals—not based on Soul, but based on their actions

UNCONSCIOUSLY EXPERIENCING THIS LANGUAGE:

Living behind a façade or a false image of yourself

Judging yourself or others for not being "Soulful" enough

Creating co-dependent relationships by seeing the essence of an individual but not taking their actions into consideration

Feeling "not good enough"

SIGNS YOU ARE ON THE PATH:

You know who you are

You compassionately explain to others what they can bring into their reality

You are in alignment with body, mind, and spirit

LANGUAGE ORIENTATION:

The *Image Maker* is Action. Your Soul has a desire to move into action first and uses the strength of knowing. It is important that you set aside time for stillness so you aren't doing just for the sake of doing. Also, too much action can be expressed in trying to control and command a situation.

ACCESSING AND ATTRACTING SUPPORT:

Caretaker (Axiom of Quest) – These individuals are the custodians of a belief, theory, person, or object. They can show the *Image Maker* how to care with proper boundaries.

Constable (Axiom of Translation) – These individuals are here to maintain peace. They can show the *Image Maker* how to resonate calm authority and be still so they can feel and see the images of their Soul and the Souls of others.

Bodybuilder (Tone) – These individuals can teach the *Image Maker* how to perceive the building blocks of form and Soul in order to understand how form and Soul fit together and see where truth can be built up.

IF YOUR BUSINESS'S AXIOM OF TRANSLATION IS IMAGE MAKER:

> You are clear what the essence of your business is and how to express that in its image
>
> You are clear that your community has a desire to know and be true to who they are
>
> You exhibit integrity and communicate the value of the business

A CHILD WHO SPEAKS THIS LANGUAGE WILL THRIVE IN AN ENVIRONMENT THAT:

> Allows them to share what they feel and see with others in an appropriate way
>
> Provides them with an understanding that not everyone can see through the hype and the fluff
>
> Provides them with experiences that allow them to express their Soul in their reality
>
> Helps them understand that it is not up to them whether or not others fulfill their potential

QUESTIONS TO ASK YOUR IMAGE MAKER:

> What of my essence is calling to be expressed in my reality?
>
> What am I projecting that is not in alignment with my true essence?

LAWMAKER

Axiom of Translation

You will be known here for creating guidelines and instituting laws. You are able to understand human nature and create principles that will protect us and allow us to evolve.

These guidelines can be thoughts, customs, beliefs, principles, or physical laws—any rule or injunction that can be obeyed to create life without struggle.

You are a master at constructing principles in order to maintain a sense of order and balance. The *Lawmaker's* goal is to construct these principles in order to allow humans to feel a sense of peace.

INFLUENTIAL WORDS:

Structure

Peace

Principle

ABILITIES AND TALENTS:

You are able to create structure that allows you and others to feel safe and peaceful

You can see how others create unnecessary structure that is unhelpful or outdated

CONSCIOUSLY EXPERIENCING THIS LANGUAGE:

Understanding that certain laws need to be flexible

Understanding that the individuals for whom laws are created are as important as the laws themselves

Updating laws and structure for your expansion as needed

UNCONSCIOUSLY EXPERIENCING THIS LANGUAGE:

Being proud and inflexible

Being over-critical of yourself and/or others

Thinking rules are more important than the reason they were created

Setting up laws and structures that are limiting or controlling

SIGNS YOU ARE ON THE PATH:

You know what laws need to be created for a life of peace

You know when to be flexible

You are open-minded

LANGUAGE ORIENTATION:

The *Lawmaker* is Action. Your Soul has a desire to move directly into action. Action out of control will result in overdoing and thinking you need to control everything and everyone.

ACCESSING AND ATTRACTING SUPPORT:

Equalizer (Axiom of Quest) – These individuals have an innate knowing of how to achieve the perfect formula for balance. They will be able to add a sense of balance and flexibility to the *Lawmaker*.

Master (Axiom of Translation) – These individuals provide the big-picture point of view. They can help the *Lawmaker* see the larger purpose of creating structure and laws for themselves and others.

Enchantress/Enchanter (Tone) – These individuals share an innate understanding of how to (Soulfully) influence and charm others. They can help the *Lawmaker* be lighter and help them learn how to explain structure to their community with ease.

IF YOUR BUSINESS'S AXIOM OF TRANSLATION IS LAWMAKER:

You need to understand when structure needs to be updated

You need to know what structure has been created and how it is being used

You need to understand how being flexible can be profitable

A CHILD WHO SPEAKS THIS LANGUAGE WILL THRIVE IN AN ENVIRONMENT THAT:

Provides them with an understanding of what their own personal laws are

Encourages and models flexibility

Provides them with an understanding of their value

Shows them compassion

QUESTIONS TO ASK YOUR LAWMAKER:

Where have I created a law that no longer benefits me?

Where am I judging myself or others?

MASTER

Axiom of Translation

You will be known here as the "Big Idea" person. You are capable of creating grand masterpieces.

You understand spiritual "needs" and provide "big ideas" that will support the spiritual growth of yourself and others.

INFLUENTIAL WORDS:

Knowledge

Expert

Universal

ABILITIES AND TALENTS:

You are able to understand and share with others big Universal themes (knowledge, growth, expansion, etc.)

You have vast knowledge and experience to share with others

You can be an "expert" in many different categories

CONSCIOUSLY EXPERIENCING THIS LANGUAGE:

Accepting the fact that you no longer need to prove you are an expert or a master

Understanding what is truly a detail

Accepting the fact that you don't have to focus on the details, and instead assigning others those tasks

Understanding and remembering that you are always a student of life

Understanding that quality, not quantity, is the sign of a true master

Being grounded in your body and allowing Soul to flow through you

Accepting your abilities to help create majestic transformations for yourself and others by truly understanding the master plan

Understanding how you and others are influenced by both outside and inside forces

UNCONSCIOUSLY EXPERIENCING THIS LANGUAGE:

Weighing yourself down with the details and getting stuck "making" those details happen

Feeling as if your body and/or your reality is limiting

Berating yourself and judging yourself for the "little things"

Doubting your ability to create a masterpiece

Feeling disconnected from the Universe/Spirit/Divine

Trying new things and gathering knowledge as a distraction or self-sabotage

Being a perfectionist

SIGNS YOU ARE ON THE PATH:

You know, accept, and value the knowledge you have

You are not trying to master everything in your life

You know your "big idea"

LANGUAGE ORIENTATION:

The *Master* is Action/Still. Your Soul has a desire to reflect prior to moving into action. It is important that you utilize the stillness to go deeper in your knowledge and to fully understand the "big picture." From there you can move into action.

ACCESSING AND ATTRACTING SUPPORT:

Equalizer (Axiom of Quest) – These individuals can teach the *Masters* how to bring balance to their mastering and to their lives.

Lawmaker (Axiom of Translation) – These individuals are "masters" at creating structures for peace. They can help the *Master* create new beliefs for self-love.

Bodybuilder (Tone) – These individuals focus on the creation of structure. They can help the *Master* construct the foundation for a "big idea."

IF YOUR BUSINESS'S AXIOM OF TRANSLATION IS MASTER:

You know what the "big idea" is and you express it clearly

You have a good support team of detail-oriented individuals (or individuals who handle the details)

You understand when to be the expert and when to seek guidance

A CHILD WHO SPEAKS THIS LANGUAGE WILL THRIVE IN AN ENVIRONMENT THAT:

Supports their thirst for knowledge

Provides them with a strategy to handle details in their life

Provides them with the tools to be comfortable with imperfection

QUESTIONS TO ASK YOUR MASTER:

What knowledge is important for me to understand in body, mind, and spirit?

What do I want to be acquainted with, or want my "students" to know, when I present the "big idea"?

What am I trying to control in my life?

MESSENGER

Axiom of Translation

You will be known here for your ingenuity, resourcefulness, and speed.

Like the Greek god Hermes, *Messengers* bring news from one source to another. You are also very good at "finding things out."

You are able to decode certain messages for certain purposes, and as a result you have great skill in guiding individuals (and yourself) from one phase of life to another.

INFLUENTIAL WORDS:

Communication

Meaning

Ingenuity

ABILITIES AND TALENTS:

You are able to read between the lines and really hear what is being said

You are able to understand the "messages" being sent to us via the Universe

CONSCIOUSLY EXPERIENCING THIS LANGUAGE:

Being clear about your own message

Being clear about what the message is and who it belongs to

Listening to your own message with love

Moving through the different forms of life easily and gracefully

UNCONSCIOUSLY EXPERIENCING THIS LANGUAGE:

Feeling misunderstood

Being confused about what message you have to offer

Spreading gossip or messages that are not of a healing nature

Rushing through life, not slowing down to "hear" the messages

Resisting change and transformation

SIGNS YOU ARE ON THE PATH:

You know and are listening to your own message

You are not rushing your experience

You communicate clearly with your higher self

LANGUAGE ORIENTATION:

The *Messenger* is Action/Still. Your Soul has a desire to reflect prior to taking action. It is important that you allow yourself the space to reflect so you can receive the messages of the Universe.

ACCESSING AND ATTRACTING SUPPORT:

Mentor (Axiom of Quest) – These individuals can guide and help the *Messenger* mentor their talents and gifts so they feel safe hearing their own message and expressing that message.

Nurturer (Axiom of Translation) – These individuals can provide the *Messenger* with a deep understanding of how to nurture and care for themselves.

Disillusionist (Tone) – These individuals can help the *Messenger* break down a view of reality that is preventing them from hearing and understanding their message(s).

IF YOUR BUSINESS'S AXIOM OF TRANSLATION IS MESSENGER:

You have established a clear message and it is communicated plainly

You are a model of that message

You are conscious of timing and do not rush products or get stuck on them

A CHILD WHO SPEAKS THIS LANGUAGE WILL THRIVE IN AN ENVIRONMENT THAT:

Provides them with the support to feel safe hearing their message and expressing it

Provides them with the safety to understand that everything happens with Divine timing

Provides them with the knowledge that not everyone wants to hear the message that is for them

QUESTIONS TO ASK YOUR MESSENGER:

What is my message?

Where am I not listening to that message?

MONK

Axiom of Translation

You will be known here for your devotion to living according to a particular rule, principle, or ideal. You can provide yourself and others with valuable insights about living and developing a spiritual life.

INFLUENTIAL WORDS:

Stillness

Beauty

Unconditional

ABILITIES AND TALENTS:

You are able to embrace the beauty and the perfection of life

You are able to grow beyond your physical body and develop your spiritual life with ease

CONSCIOUSLY EXPERIENCING THIS LANGUAGE:

Feeling the consciousness of love in your life

Embodying ideals, rules, or principles to allow yourself to feel closer to the Divine

Integrating creation with human experience

Being balanced in stillness and action

Embracing the perfection of life

Unconsciously experiencing this Language:

Feeling separate, cut off, or alone

Feeling frustrated and resentful that humans are limited

Denying your spiritual existence

Feeling stuck in the stillness

Being unbalanced and conditional

Perceiving and focusing on flaws

Signs you are on the path:

You have access to quiet and allow the room, space, and time for reflection to study and embrace the beauty of life

You are fostering this beauty by sharing it with others (via art, spirituality, truth, words, etc.)

Language Orientation:

The *Monk* is Still. Your Soul has a desire for deep reflection. It is important to set time aside for quiet. This quiet allows the *Monk* time and space to study and embrace the beauty and the perfection of life.

Accessing and Attracting Support:

Mentor (Axiom of Quest) – These individuals can guide and mentor the *Monk* in the acceptance of their need for quiet.

Partner (Axiom of Translation) – These individuals are interested in co-creative partnerships. They can help the *Monk* create balanced relationships to support who they are and what they desire.

Disillusionist (Tone) – These individuals can help the *Monk* break down the interpretation of reality that is preventing them from being comfortable with their spiritual existence.

IF YOUR BUSINESS'S AXIOM OF TRANSLATION IS MONK:

You are comfortable with the quiet times during business

You create a strategy that is balanced in stillness and action

You provide time for creative thinking

A CHILD WHO SPEAKS THIS LANGUAGE WILL THRIVE IN AN ENVIRONMENT THAT:

Provides them with a balance between quiet and social time

Provides them with an appreciation of beauty

Provides them with a spiritual foundation that will support their life purpose

QUESTIONS TO ASK YOUR MONK:

Where am I not allowing myself time to reflect?

Where can I "see" the beauty of life more fully?

Motivator

Axiom of Translation

You will be known here as an incentive-giver. You are the one people turn to in order to receive words of inspiration. Through your own personal experiences or your interpretations of others', you can provide a jumpstart to make change. You can motivate others in an area even if you do not have previous experience in that area.

Influential words:

Inspiration

Encourage

Possibilities

Abilities and talents:

You are able to add your own energy to an experience in order to empower others

You have a keen sense of what to say to individuals or a group in order to jumpstart self-discovery

Consciously experiencing this Language:

Knowing what motivates you

Motivating through love, support, and Spirit

Having contagious energy and giving people the opportunity to be more friendly, more enthusiastic and/or energetic

UNCONSCIOUSLY EXPERIENCING THIS LANGUAGE:

Motivating through fear and doubt

Being over-critical or judgmental of yourself and others

Overdoing for others and not including yourself in the equation

Not knowing what motivates you

Feeling exhausted and as if you can't ask others for help because you are always supposed to be "on"

SIGNS YOU ARE ON THE PATH:

You know how to motivate yourself through love

You are not easily influenced by "fear motivators"

You experience balance between giving and receiving

LANGUAGE ORIENTATION:

The *Motivator* is Action/Still. Your Soul has a desire to reflect prior to taking action. It is important that you allow yourself the space to feel and understand the source of your motivation.

ACCESSING AND ATTRACTING SUPPORT:

Caretaker (Axiom of Quest) – These individuals are the custodians of a belief, theory, person, or object. They can show the *Motivator* how to care with proper boundaries.

Apprentice (Axiom of Translation) – These individuals are able to translate what they learn into tangible skills. They can help the *Motivator* to appreciate the "how" of things.

Conductor (Tone) – These individuals can help the *Motivator* understand how to highlight the best in individuals.

IF YOUR BUSINESS'S AXIOM OF TRANSLATION IS MOTIVATOR:

You are clear about the source of the motivation of the business (love, joy, happiness) and are not using this talent to motivate with fear

You utilize motivaton to jumpstart, not enslave

You have set up clear boundaries for the business

A CHILD WHO SPEAKS THIS LANGUAGE WILL THRIVE IN AN ENVIRONMENT THAT:

Provides them with an understanding of what their motivation is

Provides them with the knowledge of how they can inspire and lead without control

Provides them with loving and supportive feedback

QUESTIONS TO ASK YOUR MOTIVATOR:

What is my motivation?

Where am I motivating myself or others with fear and doubt?

Nurturer

Axiom of Translation

You will be known here as a person who provides for and sustains others.

Influential words:

- Receive
- Cultivate
- Willingness

Abilities and talents:

You have a keen sense of what individuals need to be comforted

You are able to achieve a balance of both providing and receiving

Consciously experiencing this Language:

Balancing your providing with receiving, which makes you a perfect giver and receiver

Being balanced in your male and female energies

Having a structure for nurturing yourself

Allowing yourself to be nurtured

Not over-nurturing to prove your worth

Knowing and expressing your value

Setting and maintaining appropriate boundaries

UNCONSCIOUSLY EXPERIENCING THIS LANGUAGE:

Having trouble placing financial value on your nurturing

Not accepting nurturing from others

Being out of balance in your receiving and giving

Feeling tired, overworked, or unsupported

Feeling as if you always need to give in order to receive

Giving in hopes that you will receive

SIGNS YOU ARE ON THE PATH:

You know how to accept love and nurturing

You are balanced with your female and male energies

You know what you need to be nurtured

LANGUAGE ORIENTATION:

The *Nurturer* is Action/Still. Your Soul has a desire to reflect prior to taking action. If you neglect nurturing yourself, you could be paralyzed by stillness or caught in doing, doing, doing.

ACCESSING AND ATTRACTING SUPPORT:

Pioneer (Axiom of Quest) – These individuals can help the *Nurturer* understand what new roads they get to forge.

Master (Axiom of Translation) – These individuals can help guide the *Nurturer* to see the big picture of their life, letting go of the details.

Heartfelt Artist (Tone) – These individuals can help the *Nurturer* understand how to "listen" and act on their heart's guidance.

IF YOUR BUSINESS'S AXIOM OF TRANSLATION IS NURTURER:

You are clear about the compensation structure for your services/products

You have created clear boundaries so you are not over-nurturing

You are open to being supported and nurtured by other businesses

A CHILD WHO SPEAKS THIS LANGUAGE WILL THRIVE IN AN ENVIRONMENT THAT:

Provides them with an understanding of appropriate self-love and self-care

Provides them with an appropriate system of boundaries

Provides them with the understanding of what they need to feel nurtured

Provides them with the understanding that you don't always need to give in order to receive

QUESTIONS TO ASK YOUR NURTURER:

Where do I get to nurture myself?

Where am I over-nurturing others in order to prove that I am worthy?

PARTNER

Axiom of Translation

You will be known here as a sharer. You strive to understand the ways of others and of yourself in order to bring harmony to your life and the lives of others. Your focus is to co-create with yourself and others.

You can enjoy all aspects of a partnership. You are the perfect person to be on a teeter-totter (see saw) with because you not only enjoy pushing off the ground, you also enjoy flying in the air.

INFLUENTIAL WORDS:

Co-create

Balanced

Partnership

ABILITIES AND TALENTS:

You are able to create sustainable and balanced partnerships

You see the joy in every aspect of partnership

CONSCIOUSLY EXPERIENCING THIS LANGUAGE:

Understanding that you are an important part of any partnership

Being clear what partnership means to you and communicating it clearly to others

Valuing your worth and expressing it to yourself and others

Being balanced in your giving and receiving

Being in a "true" partnership with yourself

UNCONSCIOUSLY EXPERIENCING THIS LANGUAGE:

Creating co-dependent partnerships

Feeling like your life is out of balance

Feeling as if your needs are not being met

Being afraid to create and be in partnerships

Being unaware of what a "true" partnership means to you

Not communicating what a true partnership means to you

SIGNS YOU ARE ON THE PATH:

You know your meaning of "true Soulful" partnership and express it to others

You create partnerships that are balanced, equitable, and sustainable

LANGUAGE ORIENTATION:

The *Partner* is Action/Still. Your Soul has a desire to reflect prior to taking action. This will allow the *Partner* to determine how they feel, what they expect, and whether a particular "partnership" is for them.

ACCESSING AND ATTRACTING SUPPORT:

Caretaker (Axiom of Quest) – These individuals are custodians of a belief, theory, person, or object. They can show the *Partner* how to "take care of" their partnership with themselves and others.

Gardener (Axiom of Translation) – These individuals will be known here as "master planters." They can help the *Partner* understand what they need in their partnerships to help everything grow.

Agent (Tone) – These individuals are focused on action and bring about a reaction or a result. They can help the *Partner* determine what action can be taken for better partnerships.

IF YOUR BUSINESS'S AXIOM OF TRANSLATION IS PARTNER:

You have a clear definition of partnership that is expressed to everyone associated with the company

You have secure boundaries in place

You value your services and the company's worth, and you communicate that clearly

A CHILD WHO SPEAKS THIS LANGUAGE WILL THRIVE IN AN ENVIRONMENT THAT:

Provides them with the structure and models for creating healthy relationships

Provides them with tools for clear communication of expectations

Provides them with a knowledge of their worth and appropriate ways to express it

QUESTIONS TO ASK YOUR PARTNER:

Where am I not partnering with myself?

Where am I not conveying my ideal of a true partnership in a situation?

PLEASURE SEEKER

Axiom of Translation

You will be known here for your motivation for the desire of enjoyment.

INFLUENTIAL WORDS:

Pleasure

Joy

Seek

ABILITIES AND TALENTS:

You are able to bring instant joy to yourself and others

You are able to help others to create their own definition of pleasure

CONSCIOUSLY EXPERIENCING THIS LANGUAGE:

Understanding what "pleasure" means to you and your Soul

Not expressing any limiting beliefs about pleasure

Finding pleasure in the simplest tasks

Exhibiting your enjoyment of the world because you are full of joy within

Living in the present

UNCONSCIOUSLY EXPERIENCING THIS LANGUAGE:

Seeking pleasure without truly experiencing joy

Using "pleasure" to fill an empty space inside

Being controlled by your desires

Denying yourself enjoyment

Rushing through life

Living in the past or future

SIGNS YOU ARE ON THE PATH:

You have your own definition of pleasure

You feel complete and joyful within

You have made peace with your past

LANGUAGE ORIENTATION:

The *Pleasure Seeker* is Action. Your Soul has a desire to move directly into action. Action out of control will result in rushing through life and not fully embracing the pleasure you seek.

ACCESSING AND ATTRACTING SUPPORT:

Politician (Axiom of Quest) – These individuals provide others with the forum to speak their truth. They can help the *Pleasure Seeker* find outlets to express their truth.

Motivator (Axiom of Translation) – These individuals can help the *Pleasure Seeker* understand what is motivating their pleasure, either fear or joy.

Connoisseur (Tone) – These individuals are all about acceptance. They can help the *Pleasure Seeker* accept all parts of themselves–positive and negative.

IF YOUR BUSINESS'S AXIOM OF TRANSLATION IS PLEASURE SEEKER:

You need to understand what joy the company is offering

You need to have structures in place to take care of the "practical" side of running the business

You provide time for reflection to determine the vision and future of the company

A CHILD WHO SPEAKS THIS LANGUAGE WILL THRIVE IN AN ENVIRONMENT THAT:

Provides them with a balance of work and play

Provides them with a healthy definition of pleasure

Provides them with experiences of joy and fun

QUESTIONS TO ASK YOUR PLEASURE SEEKER:

What can I let go of to express and feel the joy within?

Where am I rushing through life and not practicing joy?

Problem Solver

Axiom of Translation

You will be known here for being able to "see" solutions to complex problems. You have the skill to streamline complex situations for yourself, for others, and for the world so that answers can be revealed.

Influential words:

Solution

Puzzle

Complexity

Abilities and talents:

You are able to see a solution almost immediately for any given problem

You are able to take a stand for innovative decisions that will illuminate the solution to a problem

Consciously experiencing this Language:

Understanding that not all problems can be solved immediately, and that it might take some time for the solutions to appear or be seen

Understanding that not everyone wants their problems to be solved

Knowing that no one can solve the problem of another person

Understanding when to present solutions and when to be a witness for yourself and others

Bringing awareness to your own problems and seeking assistance when you are in need of solutions

Being clear about what your problems are

UNCONSCIOUSLY EXPERIENCING THIS LANGUAGE:

Being impatient or judging others for not being able to see what you see

Feeling overwhelmed and unable to solve even the simplest of your own problems

Taking responsibility for others' problems

Being attached to the problem (which makes it hard to see or feel the solution)

Being attached to the outcome of your problem solving

SIGNS YOU ARE ON THE PATH:

You have a system in place to bring awareness to your own complex problems

You are balanced in reflection and movement

You welcome input from others

LANGUAGE ORIENTATION:

The *Problem Solver* is Action/Still. It is important that you allow for reflection and listen to your heart and Soul before moving into action.

ACCESSING AND ATTRACTING SUPPORT:

Politician (Axiom of Quest) – These individuals provide others the forum to speak their truth. They can help the *Problem Solver* with speaking up and asking for help with their own problems.

Motivator (Axiom of Translation) – These individuals can help the *Problem Solver* understand how to motivate individuals by promoting an opportunity to take action on a solution.

Industrialist (Tone) – These individuals can see how to use the mind to help create another way of being. They can help the *Problem Solver* have a productive mindset.

IF YOUR BUSINESS'S AXIOM OF TRANSLATION IS PROBLEM SOLVER:

The company clearly communicates that some problems take time to solve

The company clearly communicates what problem it is offering solutions for

The company is clear about which problems it is willing to provide guidance for

A CHILD WHO SPEAKS THIS LANGUAGE WILL THRIVE IN AN ENVIRONMENT THAT:

Provides them with tools to engage their ability to solve complex problems

Provides them with good communication skills so they can share with others what they "see"

Teaches patience and compassion

QUESTIONS TO ASK YOUR PROBLEM SOLVER:

How can I look at this problem from another point of view?

Where am I attached to this problem or its solution?

PURVEYOR

Axiom of Translation

You will be known here for your ability to secure and provide. You have unlimited access to networks and contacts in order to secure resources, goods, and/or services.

INFLUENTIAL WORDS:

Unlimited Resources

Community/Contacts

Sharing

ABILITIES AND TALENTS:

You are able to see what resources, services, etc., individuals could utilize

You are able to connect with many different types of people and groups

CONSCIOUSLY EXPERIENCING THIS LANGUAGE:

Knowing what you "need" and including yourself in the equation

Providing resources to others without attachment

Providing resources, goods, and services to others in a balanced way, both giving and receiving

Providing for community members who are open to receiving

Knowing that providing is just another form of sharing

UNCONSCIOUSLY EXPERIENCING THIS LANGUAGE:

Begging, borrowing, or "stealing" to ensure that other people's needs are met (this keeps the victim energy going)

Providing only for your own needs

Providing only for others and not meeting your own needs

Being unaware of your needs, wants, and desires

Feeling exhausted, as if your needs, wants, and desires are not being met

SIGNS YOU ARE ON THE PATH:

You know your own needs, wants, and desires

You include yourself in the equation of giving and receiving

You are in joyful service

LANGUAGE ORIENTATION:

The *Purveyor* is Action. Your Soul has a desire to move into action. It is important that you take time to reflect and understand the "big picture" so you aren't over servicing or moving into self-indulgence.

ACCESSING AND ATTRACTING SUPPORT:

Counselor (Axiom of Quest) – These individuals can provide counsel and strategies to help the *Purveyor* understand their needs, wants, and desires.

Goddess (Axiom of Translation) – These individuals radiate female energy. They can help the *Purveyor* open up to receiving.

Dionysian (Tone) – These individuals have a zest for life. They can help the *Purveyor* experience the richness of life instead of seeing it as an exchange of resources.

IF YOUR BUSINESS'S AXIOM OF TRANSLATION IS PURVEYOR:

You are clear about what goods, products, and services you are providing

You are clear about the compensation for what you provide

You have clear boundaries and are in joyful service as you help others through your connections

A CHILD WHO SPEAKS THIS LANGUAGE WILL THRIVE IN AN ENVIRONMENT THAT:

Provides them with an understanding of the differences between needs, wants, and desires

Provides them with the knowledge and understanding of "joyful service"

Nurtures their ability to connect individuals with resources

QUESTIONS TO ASK YOUR PURVEYOR:

What is my Soul's desire?

Who or what resource do I know that can help or guide me to being in alignment with this desire?

RAINMAKER

Axiom of Translation

You will be known here for your exceptional ability to attract what you desire simply by stating it. You are able to help activate the power of manifestation in yourself and others.

There are a number of ways that you can do this: rituals, thoughts, visualizations, affirmations, intention setting, etc.

INFLUENTIAL WORDS:

Manifestation

Abundance

Attraction

ABILITIES AND TALENTS:

You are able to instantly manifest

You are able to create out of thin air

CONSCIOUSLY EXPERIENCING THIS LANGUAGE:

Understanding that you are a conduit for Soulful desire

Co-creating with the Universe

Not being attached to manifestation

Knowing that your reality is a reflection of how you feel

Knowing that the only true reality is that you are one with the Divine

UNCONSCIOUSLY EXPERIENCING THIS LANGUAGE:

Allowing limiting beliefs to block your powers of manifestation

Looking outside yourself for validation

Manifesting material things in order to feel complete and whole

Manifesting non-nurturing situations or a life full of struggle

SIGNS YOU ARE ON THE PATH:

You know what you truly want to manifest (body, mind, and spirit)

You have no attachment to manifestation

LANGUAGE ORIENTATION:

The *Rainmaker* is Action. Your Soul has a desire to take action. You need to set aside time to be Still in order to really tune into Soulful desires, and to receive them.

ACCESSING AND ATTRACTING SUPPORT:

Negotiator (Axiom of Quest) – These individuals help create new deals. They can help *Rainmakers* understand where they are manifesting situations that are not nurturing to their lives.

Nurturer (Axiom of Translation) – These individuals can help the *Rainmaker* learn how to love and nurture themselves.

Deliberator (Tone) – These individuals are amazing decision-makers. They can help *Rainmakers* make better free-will choices.

IF YOUR BUSINESS'S AXIOM OF TRANSLATION IS RAINMAKER:

You need to make sure you have a clear revenue stream

You need to make sure you have a clear sense of what resources the company gets to manifest

You need to make sure you release attachment to the outcome of the sales transaction

A CHILD WHO SPEAKS THIS LANGUAGE WILL THRIVE IN AN ENVIRONMENT THAT:

Instills a strong sense of self-love and confidence

Provides tools for determining the difference between a want, a need, and a desire

Provides them with a healthy relationship with money and the material world

QUESTIONS TO ASK YOUR RAINMAKER:

Where can I let go of attachment in this situation?

What do I intend to manifest in this situation?

SEXTANT

Axiom of Translation

You will be known here for your innate ability to understand and explain exactly where you and others are on the journey.

Like the sextant instrument, used to determine latitude and longitude by measuring the angular distances of the sun, moon, and stars, you have a knowing (innate hearing, seeing, and understanding) that allows you to pinpoint an individual's current place on their Soul's journey.

INFLUENTIAL WORDS:

Trust

Journey

Path

ABILITIES AND TALENTS:

You are able to understand where others are on their journey and provide them with Soulful guidance to help them in their current position

You are able to experience the joy of the journey

CONSCIOUSLY EXPERIENCING THIS LANGUAGE:

Knowing your exact position in your life and on your journey

Trusting that you are receiving all the information to help guide you on your journey

Understanding that the journey is the reward, not the destination

Knowing that there is never an end to the journey, only rest stops along the way

Conducting your own journey with joy and grace

Providing information to others about their location on their journey without attachment

Unconsciously experiencing this Language:

Feeling distracted and lost, as if you don't have a sense of direction

Being filled with mistrust

Judging your own or another person's journey

Feeling judgmental about how much progress has been made

Being too focused on the end result

Signs you are on the path:

You know your place on the path

You live without resentment or judgment about your own journey or the journey of others

Language Orientation:

The *Sextant* is Action/Still. Your Soul has a desire to move into action after reflecting. The reflection or stillness is important for the *Sextant* to understand where they are on the journey, and to understand Divinely inspired action.

Accessing and Attracting Support:

Negotiator (Axiom of Quest) – These individuals are master deal-makers. They can help the *Sextant* create better deals for themselves.

Master (Axiom of Translation) – These individuals are able to see the "big picture." They can help the *Sextant* understand the big picture instead of getting distracted by the details.

Closer (Tone) – These individuals can teach the *Sextant* how to understand certain details in order to bring forth conclusions, making it easier to move forward in the journey.

IF YOUR BUSINESS'S AXIOM OF TRANSLATION IS SEXTANT:

You are clear that the company has its own journey

You accept the journey of the company

You clearly communicate to clients/customers how your business helps them understand their journey

You have clear intentions in place but do not run the company by focusing on goals alone

A CHILD WHO SPEAKS THIS LANGUAGE WILL THRIVE IN AN ENVIRONMENT THAT:

Provides them with an understanding of how to accept their journey

Celebrates enjoyment and happiness

Provides them with a balanced way of setting goals and intentions

QUESTIONS TO ASK YOUR SEXTANT:

What is preventing me from understanding my journey?

How can I experience the joy of my journey more?

Sitting Buddha

Axiom of Translation

You will be known as pure stillness. You will be known here for your quiet wisdom, for showing yourself and others the beauty of the circles of life.

Influential words:

Stillness

Space

Wisdom

Abilities and talents:

You are able to create a safe space for others to express themselves

You are able to share wisdom to help yourself and others move through the circles of life

Consciously experiencing this Language:

Treating yourself with love and respect for who you are

Accepting the stillness and drawing strength from it

Creating the space for your own self-expression

Accepting the circles of life and being patient with change and transformation

Sharing your wisdom without attachment

Operating in present time

UNCONSCIOUSLY EXPERIENCING THIS LANGUAGE:

Believing or acting as if you have power over the circles of life

Being uncomfortable with the stillness

Operating from a place of ego or fear

Insisting that your knowledge is the right wisdom for all

Finding yourself living in the past or the future

SIGNS YOU ARE ON THE PATH:

You are comfortable in the stillness

You are full of acceptance and love for yourself

You are living in the present moment

LANGUAGE ORIENTATION:

The *Sitting Buddha* is Still. It is important that you allow for reflection and learn how to draw strength from reflection, meditation, or prayer.

ACCESSING AND ATTRACTING SUPPORT:

Prophet (Axiom of Quest) – These individuals know not only the message but also the structure for that message. They can help the *Sitting Buddha* with structure for self-expression.

Purveyor (Axiom of Translation) – These individuals have access to an unlimited supply of resources. They can help the *Sitting Buddha* receive the resources they need to move from stillness into action.

Captain (Tone) – These individuals can help focus a group for a certain task. They can help the *Sitting Buddha* share their wisdom.

IF YOUR BUSINESS'S AXIOM OF TRANSLATION IS SITTING BUDDHA:

The company understands what wisdom it is offering to others

The company has clear structures in place for reflection

The company is clear what "space" it offers people to express themselves, and it expresses itself as well

A CHILD WHO SPEAKS THIS LANGUAGE WILL THRIVE IN AN ENVIRONMENT THAT:

Provides them with opportunities to be still

Provides them with opportunities for self-expression

Provides them with tools for patience and compassion

QUESTIONS TO ASK YOUR SITTING BUDDHA:

Why am I afraid to be in the stillness?

What wisdom do I have to share with myself and others?

STRATEGIST

Axiom of Translation

You will be known here for creating methods to obtain a specific goal or result.

INFLUENTIAL WORDS:

Method

Maneuver

Approach

ABILITIES AND TALENTS:

You are able to design and create clever and unusual systems for achieving an objective

You are able to understand how all the different tactics link together to create a strategy

CONSCIOUSLY EXPERIENCING THIS LANGUAGE:

Understanding the difference between a tactic and a strategy

Understanding your part in the strategy

Being without attachment; not trying to force or control how the pieces come together

Understanding that strategies have to be flexible

Accepting your innovative talents

Checking within to determine what in your own strategy can be updated

Unconsciously experiencing this Language:

Being manipulative

Hiding out or withdrawing

Not participating in your own strategy

Feeling as if you don't have a voice

Feeling misunderstood

Feeling unclear about the goal or objective of the strategy

Signs you are on the path:

You have a strategy in place for your own life

You are accepting of your innovative talents

You are living in the present moment

Language Orientation:

The *Strategist* is Action. Your Soul has a desire to move into action first and foremost. It is suggested that you allow additional time so that you can understand more of a strategy's moving parts.

Accessing and Attracting Support:

Mentor (Axiom of Quest) – These individuals provide guidance and mentorship for others. They can help the *Strategist* understand what they need for their own strategy.

Purveyor (Axiom of Translation) – These individuals have access to an unlimited supply of resources. They can help the *Strategist* find resources for their plans and strategies.

Conductor (Tone) – These individuals are all about acceptance. They can help the *Strategist* accept their gifts and talents.

IF YOUR BUSINESS'S AXIOM OF TRANSLATION IS STRATEGIST:

The company is clear about its objectives

The company has innovative systems in place

The company is updating its strategy on a frequent basis, allowing for more information to build on the strategy

A CHILD WHO SPEAKS THIS LANGUAGE WILL THRIVE IN AN ENVIRONMENT THAT:

Provides them with opportunities to express their own kinds of innovation

Provides them with a way to work out problems for themselves

Encourages and supports flexibility

QUESTIONS TO ASK YOUR STRATEGIST:

What is the goal or objective of this strategy?

Where am I holding myself back in this situation?

SUN

Axiom of Translation

You will be known here as an individual who is rising to enlightenment. You can instantly bring light and life to a darkened area.

You help yourself and others rise to enlightenment and know that the light is from within, not from without.

INFLUENTIAL WORDS:

Light

Freedom

Joy

ABILITIES AND TALENTS:

You are able to find beauty in the mud and light in a dark hole

You are able to feel and understand the "sunny side" of every situation

CONSCIOUSLY EXPERIENCING THIS LANGUAGE:

Focusing on expansion without judgment

Being full of radiance and vitality

Understanding and living in your personal power

Enjoying life and allowing that to spill over to others

Giving others the opportunity to rise to their full potential

UNCONSCIOUSLY EXPERIENCING THIS LANGUAGE:

Hiding your light

Giving up hope

Feeling stuck or drained

Feeling alone and unsupported

Living in the shadow of someone or something else

Judging yourself or others

SIGNS YOU ARE ON THE PATH:

You are living and expressing your own personal power

You understand what you get to let go of in order to continue rising to enlightenment

LANGUAGE ORIENTATION:

The *Sun* is Action/Still. Your Soul has a desire to reflect prior to moving into action. It is important that you utilize the stillness to feel the joy and light inside of you prior to moving into action.

ACCESSING AND ATTRACTING SUPPORT:

Politician (Axiom of Quest) – These individuals provide a forum for others to speak their truth. They can help the *Sun* accept their power.

Motivator (Axiom of Translation) – These individuals can help the *Sun* understand what is motivating them, either fear or love.

Firemaker (Tone) – These individuals help others ignite their passions. They can help the *Sun* understand what they are passionate about.

IF YOUR BUSINESS'S AXIOM OF TRANSLATION IS SUN:

You have clear boundaries with clients

You know what enlightenment you are offering to your clients

You have clear systems in place for support

A CHILD WHO SPEAKS THIS LANGUAGE WILL THRIVE IN AN ENVIRONMENT THAT:

Provides them with a strong sense of self

Provides them with clear boundaries

Provides them with an understanding of their gifts and talents

QUESTIONS TO ASK YOUR SUN:

Where am I giving away my power?

Where can I step more into the light in this situation?

TEACHER

Axiom of Translation

You will be known here as a giver of knowledge. Your focus is to take complex subjects and present them in a way that others can understand and digest so they can incorporate them into their own lives.

INFLUENTIAL WORDS:

Teach

Inspire

Knowledge

ABILITIES AND TALENTS:

You are able to take complex subjects and present them in a way that others can understand and assimilate

You are able to inspire

CONSCIOUSLY EXPERIENCING THIS LANGUAGE:

Understanding that the impact you have on your "students" is Divinely guided

Constantly learning and being open to receiving information

Inspiring yourself as well as others

Understanding how to provide information in ways that your "students" can assimilate it

Knowing what you wish to create for yourself, and inspiring others to create for themselves through knowledge

Understanding information on multiple levels

Teaching your "students" and also learning from them

UNCONSCIOUSLY EXPERIENCING THIS LANGUAGE:

Trying to create others in your own image

Presenting the information in a dogmatic way

Being fearful that the "student" will know more than the teacher

Having a "know-it-all" attitude

Feeling as if you are failing if your students don't seem to "get it" right away

SIGNS YOU ARE ON THE PATH:

You are open to receiving new information

You not only inspire others, you also inspire yourself

LANGUAGE ORIENTATION:

The *Teacher* is Action/Still. Your Soul has a desire to reflect prior to moving into action. It is important that you utilize the stillness to integrate knowledge, and release judgment and attachment, before presenting that material to others.

ACCESSING AND ATTRACTING SUPPORT:

Politician (Axiom of Quest) – These individuals provide a forum for others to speak their truth. They will be able to help the *Teacher* speak their truth with unconditional love, which will help them inspire their students.

Nurturer (Axiom of Translation) – These individuals can help the *Teacher* understand when they are unbalanced in their giving and receiving.

Connoisseur (Tone) – These individuals prefer to go through life full of acceptance. They can help the *Teacher* accept their abilities and let go of attachment to what their "students" do with that information.

IF YOUR BUSINESS'S AXIOM OF TRANSLATION IS TEACHER:

Your company is clear about what knowledge it is presenting to others

Your company has a structure in place for continuing education

Your company has a clear policy in place for client expectations

A CHILD WHO SPEAKS THIS LANGUAGE WILL THRIVE IN AN ENVIRONMENT THAT:

Provides them with opportunities to learn new material

Provides them with role models that are inspirational

Provides them with the chance to discover what subjects they are passionate about

QUESTIONS TO ASK YOUR TEACHER:

Where am I a teacher in this situation, and where am I a student?

What inspires me?

TEACHER OF INTEGRITY

Axiom of Translation

You will be known here as honest and a holder of strict codes. You can immediately see whether someone is lying, untrustworthy, out of integrity, or expressing love conditionally.

You spend your life "walking the talk" and taking the high road.

INFLUENTIAL WORDS:

Truthfulness

Honesty

Unconditional

ABILITIES AND TALENTS:

You can see whether someone is expressing conditional or unconditional love for themselves

You have the strength to "take the high road"

CONSCIOUSLY EXPERIENCING THIS LANGUAGE:

Accepting that you lead by example

Understanding that you will be able to provide others with the pathway to integrity and doing it without attachment

Understanding that not everyone "wants" to be in integrity

Attracting individuals who do want to be in integrity

Having intimate relationships with individuals whose words and actions measure up

Understanding that you are both a teacher and a student

UNCONSCIOUSLY EXPERIENCING THIS LANGUAGE:

Judging yourself or others for being out of integrity

Having problems with authority and creating conflicts

Taking peoples' reactions personally if they do not resonate with you

Having standards too high for anyone to achieve

Feeling alone or unsupported

Having high expectations of others without letting them know of those expectations

Creating relationships that are out of integrity; feeling alone in these relationships

SIGNS YOU ARE ON THE PATH:

You are walking your talk

You focus on your own journey

You have created supportive, healthy relationships

LANGUAGE ORIENTATION:

The *Teacher of Integrity* is Action. Your Soul has a desire to move directly into action. This can cause you to judge without knowing all the elements of a situation.

ACCESSING AND ATTRACTING SUPPORT:

Equalizer (Axiom of Quest) – These individuals can help the *Teacher of Integrity* understand how to maintain balance and live without judgment.

Motivator (Axiom of Translation) – These individuals can help the *Teacher of Integrity* understand what their motivation is, and why.

Graceful Warrior (Tone) – These individuals can help the *Teacher of Integrity* understand honor. They can help the *Teacher of Integrity* not just talk the talk, but also walk the walk.

IF YOUR BUSINESS'S AXIOM OF TRANSLATION IS TEACHER OF INTEGRITY:

You are clear that the company's actions and words measure up

You have a clear ethics policy

You have accepted that you are a leader who will always take the high road

A CHILD WHO SPEAKS THIS LANGUAGE WILL THRIVE IN AN ENVIRONMENT THAT:

Provides them with a good set of values and ethics

Provides them with the understanding that not everyone wants to be shown the path of integrity

Provides them with the understanding that they will be the one to take the high road, and that sometimes it feels uncomfortable or difficult to do that

QUESTIONS TO ASK YOUR TEACHER OF INTEGRITY:

Where am I out of integrity?

Where am I judging this situation?

How can I move into and the consciousness of love in this situation?

Transformer

Axiom of Translation

You will be known here for how you transform yourself and others.

Influential words:

Alter

Insight

Transform

Abilities and talents:

You are able to transform information into insight

You are able to show others how to access the source of powerful transformation inside of them

Consciously experiencing this Language:

Co-creating with the Divine to change from ego-driven to spirit-driven with support for ego (Divine action)

Knowing what in your own ego gets to be transmuted to allow spirit to flow with ease

Creating relationships and exchanges that are equal and balanced

Being unafraid of change or transformation

Understanding that within us we have a source of great transformation

Unconsciously experiencing this Language:

Being ego-driven by ignoring spirit

Determining for others what they "need" to change

Avoiding your own transformation

Fearing change

Creating uneven exchanges

Signs you are on the path:

You know what you want to transform in your own life

You are living in Divine action

Language Orientation:

The *Transformer* is Action/Still. Your Soul has a desire to reflect prior to moving into action. This allows you to understand what and how something can be transformed.

Accessing and Attracting Support:

Prophet (Axiom of Quest) – These individuals understand the structure needed to deliver a message. They can help the *Transformer* understand what might be needed in their own transformational process.

Messenger (Axiom of Translation) – These individuals hear the messages of the Universe. They can help the *Transformer* understand their own inner messages.

Diplomat (Tone) – These individuals help to create new relationships of love. They can help the *Transformer* create balanced relationships.

IF YOUR BUSINESS'S AXIOM OF TRANSLATION IS TRANSFORMER:

The company is clear what transformation it is offering

The company has a clear compensation system in place

The company has systems in place for its own growth and change

A CHILD WHO SPEAKS THIS LANGUAGE WILL THRIVE IN AN ENVIRONMENT THAT:

Provides them with a space to express their knowledge and insight

Provides them with a structure for ego that is healthy and supportive

Allows them to change their mind

QUESTIONS TO ASK YOUR TRANSFORMER:

What would I like to transform in my life?

What part is my ego playing in this situation?

Troubadour

Axiom of Translation

You will be known here for how you sing the stories and praises of yourself and others. You share with the world the good deeds and triumphs of individuals so that we may all benefit and grow.

Influential words:

Honor

Capture

Stories

Abilities and talents:

You are able to chronicle the life of someone (including yourself) so that others understand their impact on the Universe

You can bring stories to life

Consciously experiencing this Language:

Co-creating with the Divine to relay "stories" of Soulful human expression of all kinds

Knowing which "story" gets to be told when

Understanding what "story" you are sharing about yourself

Basing your stories on Divine truth and inspiration

Surrendering to the creative process to allow the story to take shape

Being comfortable in the spotlight

Creating new stories for yourself every day

UNCONSCIOUSLY EXPERIENCING THIS LANGUAGE:

Not knowing how to praise yourself

Experiencing low self-esteem

Letting your ego draft the stories and praises

Avoiding attention and the spotlight

Using your own "story" as a way to stay hidden and small

SIGNS YOU ARE ON THE PATH:

You know your own story and are without judgment of it

You are stepping boldly into the spotlight

LANGUAGE ORIENTATION:

The *Troubadour* is Action/Still. Your Soul has a desire to reflect prior to moving into action. This allows you to listen to Divine inspiration to create the story.

ACCESSING AND ATTRACTING SUPPORT:

Peacemaker (Axiom of Quest) – These individuals help themselves and others feel the sense of peace within. They can help the *Troubadour* be peaceful in the spotlight.

Partner (Axiom of Translation) – These individuals are experts on creating sustainable partnerships. They can teach the *Troubadour* how to partner with themselves to tell their own story.

Diplomat (Tone) – These individuals help to create new relationships of love. They can help the *Troubadour* create a deeper, more loving relationship with themselves.

IF YOUR BUSINESS'S AXIOM OF TRANSLATION IS TROUBADOUR:

The company's story is clearly stated

The company is clear about what story it is helping its client tell

The company has a strategy for being in the "spotlight"

A CHILD WHO SPEAKS THIS LANGUAGE WILL THRIVE IN AN ENVIRONMENT THAT:

Provides them with the opportunity to experience the spotlight in a positive way

Provides them with opportunities to appropriately share their storytelling talents

Provides them with opportunities to explore their creative talents

QUESTIONS TO ASK YOUR TROUBADOUR:

What is my own story that I would like to tell?

Where am I using a painful story of my past to stay hidden in the illusion of safety?

WANDERER

Axiom of Translation

You will be known as a great traveler. Like a great traveler, you can go from place to place, person to person, and culture to culture while embracing the knowledge gained from each trip.

Your journey or course of action might seem illogical to others and yet perfectly seamless to you. You can easily transplant yourself and experience something new.

INFLUENTIAL WORDS:

Journey

Knowledge

Community

ABILITIES AND TALENTS:

You are able to share with others the great wisdom from your journeys in order to better their lives

You are able to feel at home no matter where you go

CONSCIOUSLY EXPERIENCING THIS LANGUAGE:

Understanding what wisdom from your journeys to use, and when

Acting without attachment when it is time to move onto something new

Understanding that each leg of your journey is vital to the next leg of your journey

Finding support and community wherever you go

UNCONSCIOUSLY EXPERIENCING THIS LANGUAGE:

Firmly planting yourself into an environment and being afraid to move on to the next journey of your life

Being afraid to place roots

Mourning every loss from your past

Feeling lost and without community

SIGNS YOU ARE ON THE PATH:

You know when to move and when to plant roots

You let go of attachments along the journey

LANGUAGE ORIENTATION:

The *Wanderer* is Action/Still. Your Soul has a desire to reflect prior to moving into action. This allows you to fully understand when it is "time" to move onto the next journey.

ACCESSING AND ATTRACTING SUPPORT:

Negotiator (Axiom of Quest) – These individuals are all about creating win-win deals for themselves and others. They can help *Wanderers* understand where they need a new agreement with themselves.

Monk (Axiom of Translation) – These individuals understand beauty and stillness. They can help the *Wanderer* understand how they can be more comfortable in the stillness.

Capitalist (Tone) – These individuals prefer abundance. They can help the *Wanderer* balance giving and receiving.

IF YOUR BUSINESS'S AXIOM OF TRANSLATION IS WANDERER:

The company is clear about what information it is sharing with others

The company has systems and structures in place to gather knowledge and experiences

The company is balanced and has a place in the community

A CHILD WHO SPEAKS THIS LANGUAGE WILL THRIVE IN AN ENVIRONMENT THAT:

Provides them with opportunities to explore new things

Provides them with opportunities to experience different types of community

Provides them with opportunities to gain and share knowledge of their journeys

QUESTIONS TO ASK YOUR WANDERER:

What am I learning from this part of my journey?

How can I share this knowledge with another?

Weight Carrier

Axiom of Translation

You will be known here for having the capacity to carry the weight of the world on your shoulders without feeling the burden of the load.

Influential words:

Strength

Substance

Influence

Abilities and Talents:

You are able to support others in regaining their strength

You have an unlimited source of compassion

Consciously experiencing this Language:

Having the strength to help others weather any storm or shoulder any burden

Being a resource for comfort and knowledge

Understanding the unlimited resources we have to help us move through anything

Trusting the Divine to help lift any burden

Knowing when to let go of weight that is not yours to carry

Having appropriate boundaries

UNCONSCIOUSLY EXPERIENCING THIS LANGUAGE:

Playing the professional victim

Not taking responsibility for your own life

Blaming others for the weight you carry

Constantly seeking validation for your strength and courage by placing yourself in situations where others will feel sympathetic towards you

Being in servitude

SIGNS YOU ARE ON THE PATH:

You periodically let go of what is not serving you

You are full of compassion for yourself

LANGUAGE ORIENTATION:

The *Weight Carrier* is Still. Your Soul has a desire for reflection. It is suggested that you utilize this stillness to listen to yourself and the Divine to determine what weight you get to let go of for you to feel your own strength.

ACCESSING AND ATTRACTING SUPPORT:

Counselor (Axiom of Quest) – These individuals provide specific counsel. They can help the *Weight Carriers* understand how the energy of victimhood is being expressed in their lives.

Image Maker (Axiom of Translation) – These individuals provide opportunities to bring the Soul's potential into reality. They can help the *Weight Carrier* tap into the gifts of their Soul.

Conductor (Tone) – These individuals help bring out the best in themselves and others. They can help the *Weight Carrier* highlight their own best in order to bring forth confidence and feelings of value.

IF YOUR BUSINESS'S AXIOM OF TRANSLATION IS WEIGHT CARRIER:

You have clear boundaries with clients

You know what "weight" you are offering to help carry

Your company has a clear compensation plan in place, and enforces it

A CHILD WHO SPEAKS THIS LANGUAGE WILL THRIVE IN AN ENVIRONMENT THAT:

Provides them with a strong sense of self

Provides them with clear boundaries

Provides them with a balanced understanding of giving and receiving

QUESTIONS TO ASK YOUR WEIGHT CARRIER:

Where am I looking outside of myself for validation?

Where am I playing the victim?

CHAPTER 7:

Tone – Your Soulful Personality

You will learn in this chapter:

- The different Tones

- How to collaborate with your Tone

- Questions for your Tone

Tone

This Soul Language category provides insight about your Soulful personality. Expressing your Tone consciously means experiencing your Soul's personality unconditionally and without judgment.

Your Tone describes how you prefer to go through life–it is your preference. Some of us, like the *Graceful Warrior*, prefer to go through life with grace, courage, and action. Others, like the *Investigator*, feel a desire to study, examine the details, and ask questions. The Tone is also where the ego spends a lot of time expressing itself. We tend to judge ego, but please remember that it has a good side. Without ego you would be sitting on your couch, feeling and thinking your big thoughts, without ever going out and acting on them. But sometimes the free-will choices we make based on ego can result in misalignment or struggle.

Collaborating with your Tone

It is valuable to create a deeper relationship with your Tone because it enables you to create more powerful choices and relationships. By connecting with your Tone, you can develop a deeper sense of your own preferences and strengths in order to accept and express yourself more fully.

Understanding and bringing consciousness to this Language allows you to:

- Take life a lot less personally

- Exercise ego consciously

- Have a new way to be compassionate towards yourself and others

- Live less in fear and more in the power of truth

Intention Setting

Create a conscious connection with your Tone and complete the sentence below:

My personal intention today is to feel...

Want to add additional power to your intention? Write it down in your journal and say it out loud.

Questions for your Tone

Create a conscious connection with your Tone. Then ask these questions to initiate a conversation:

What do I get to accept, allow, activate or let go of in order to avoid the tendency for ego to sabotage?

What action can I take today?

What action can I take on a daily basis in order to express ego positively in creating the life I truly desire?

How is ego fooling me to live in the illusion of safety?

Where can I let go of control and know I'm being supported?

What are some triggers for self-sabotage that I can be aware of?

How will accepting my own preferences help me feel more at peace?

How can I utilize ego to help me live the life I desire?

How am I taking responsibility for other people's feelings or actions?

What do I need to take responsibility for in my own life?

What fear stops me on a daily basis, and why?

See the individual Soul Language definitions for additional questions specific to your Tone.

Tone Language Definitions

There are 55 Languages in this category. We usually spend a lot of time trying to wrestle with or blame ego. When you embrace ego as a part of your nature and something that is working to keep you safe, you can compassionately love that part of you. Once love (non-judgment) is added to a relationship, the nature of that relationship changes.

Ego only wishes to be acknowledged. The key here is to acknowledge it without supporting or enabling this part of you to live in fear and doubt.

AGENT

Tone

You prefer to go through life with focused action to achieve a specific result.

You are able to bring about a reaction or result that forever changes all parties involved.

INFLUENTIAL WORDS:

Action

Outcome

Achievement

ABILITIES AND TALENTS:

You are able to bring about results

You have a keen awareness about what actions lead to what results

CONSCIOUSLY EXPERIENCING THIS LANGUAGE:

Understanding which action needs to be facilitated, and when

Taking action that is Divinely inspired

Knowing what specific result you desire

Creating actions based in the consciousness of love

Unconsciously experiencing this Language:

Giving away your power to act

Taking power away from another (either knowingly or unknowingly)

Feeling stuck because you are unsure about what action to take

Judging your own actions or another's

Signs you are on the path:

Your actions are guided by Divine inspiration

You have created appropriate boundaries

Language Orientation:

The *Agent* is Action. Your Soul has a desire to move directly into action. It is important that you pause to understand what the Divinely inspired action is. This will help the *Agent* create the desired results.

Accessing and Attracting Support:

Observer (Axiom of Quest) – These individuals can help the *Agent* observe where action can be taken and where stillness is required.

Messenger (Axiom of Translation) – These individuals can guide the *Agent* during transitions, where sometimes no action is required.

Carter (Tone) – These individuals can help the *Agent* to listen to their heart and hear their Soul.

IF YOUR BUSINESS'S TONE IS AGENT:

You have a strategic plan in place

You have a clear understanding about the desired results for the company

You have an appropriate structure for command of power

A CHILD WHO SPEAKS THIS LANGUAGE WILL THRIVE IN AN ENVIRONMENT THAT:

Provides them with a balanced set of ethics

Provides them with the power to take appropriate action

Provides them with a strong sense of confidence

QUESTIONS TO ASK YOUR AGENT:

What is the Divinely inspired action in this situation?

Where am I acting out of fear?

ALCHEMIST

Tone

You prefer to go through life by combining the different elements of life to help create new situations and transformations. You bring together combinations that assist others and yourself in achieving an outcome of greater value, "making dreams come true."

You prefer to understand the inner workings of life in order to help a transformation take place, and you are able to access the inner workings of others to assist in their transformation.

INFLUENTIAL WORDS:

Transformation

Change

Magic

ABILITIES AND TALENTS:

You are able to be an instrument of change and transformation

You are able to understand situations and people deeply

CONSCIOUSLY EXPERIENCING THIS LANGUAGE:

Being guided by the Divine to create new situations

Living in balance and harmony with yourself and the world around you

Creating your alchemy in accordance with free will

Knowing that the ability to transform is within you and everyone else on the planet

Understanding your own dreams and desires

UNCONSCIOUSLY EXPERIENCING THIS LANGUAGE:

Manipulating the world around you to generate what you want

Being unaware of your dreams

Being unaware of what you are transforming and changing

Feeling superior to others

Judging yourself or others

SIGNS YOU ARE ON THE PATH:

You know what your dreams are and continue to create your big vision

You are in balance and in alignment

LANGUAGE ORIENTATION:

The *Alchemist* is Action/Still. Your Soul has a desire to reflect prior to taking action. It is important that you access the stillness to really hear Divine guidance and understand your personal intention in creating transformation for each situation.

ACCESSING AND ATTRACTING SUPPORT:

Politician (Axiom of Quest) – These individuals provide others with a forum to speak their truth. They can help the *Alchemist* understand and speak their truth, which will help to avoid manipulation of other people's free will.

Nurturer (Axiom of Translation) – These individuals understand the balance of giving and receiving. They can help the *Alchemist* understand how they would like to be nurtured.

Olympian (Tone) – These individuals are interested in bringing out the best in human kind. They can help the *Alchemist* see the best in others, which will help release judgment and feelings of superiority.

IF YOUR BUSINESS'S TONE IS ALCHEMIST:

You are clear what transformation you are offering your community

You do not promise the impossible

The company has a clear mission and direction (and this is being updated on an on-going basis)

A CHILD WHO SPEAKS THIS LANGUAGE WILL THRIVE IN AN ENVIRONMENT THAT:

Provides them with a sense that the world is a magical place

Provides them with a deep respect for themselves and others

Provides them with a sense that dreams are possible

QUESTIONS TO ASK YOUR ALCHEMIST:

Where would I like to create transformation for myself?

Who or what am I trying to manipulate?

ANALYST

Tone

You prefer to go through life understanding the nature of things, determining the relationship between their essential features and the rest of the world.

INFLUENTIAL WORDS:

Learn

Analyze

Examine

ABILITIES AND TALENTS:

You are able to take complex concepts and relate them to basic ones

You are able to divide things into separate elements that can be understood in a more complete way

CONSCIOUSLY EXPERIENCING THIS LANGUAGE:

Understanding both the physical and non-physical (emotional/spiritual) aspects of what you are studying

Understanding how the inner workings of what you are studying fit together

Understanding how what you are studying fits into the "big picture"

Leading with your heart; not letting your mind run the show

Combining study with experience

Finding balance between intuition and analysis

Unconsciously experiencing this Language:

Focusing solely on the data, ignoring how it all relates

Over-analyzing

Leading with your mind instead of your heart

Focusing on one element and not seeing how it fits into the "big picture"

Getting stuck on studying and being afraid to experience

Signs you are on the path:

You are creating your "big picture"

Your mind is following your heart

Language Orientation:

The *Analyst* is Action. Your Soul has a desire to move directly into action. If you do not allow yourself to pause and reflect to understand how all of the parts you are studying fit into the "big picture," you could spend your whole life studying and not experiencing life.

Accessing and Attracting Support:

Prophet (Axiom of Quest) – These individuals not only understand the messages of the Universe, they understand how it all fits together. They can help the *Analyst* to better understand the "big picture" better.

Lawmaker (Axiom of Translation) – These individuals help create structures for peace. They can help the *Analyst* create new beliefs that will help their mind follow their heart.

Captain (Tone) – These individuals are in charge of a group. They can help the *Analyst* harness the power of others to help with the "big picture".

IF YOUR BUSINESS'S TONE IS ANALYST:

You understand the "big picture" and how all the parts of the company fit into that picture

You provide your audience with a clear understanding of the heart of the company

You have appropriate systems in place to analyze your data

A CHILD WHO SPEAKS THIS LANGUAGE WILL THRIVE IN AN ENVIRONMENT THAT:

Supports them in understanding their inner world and emotions

Provides them with "big-picture" thinking

Provides them with the safety to experience life

QUESTIONS TO ASK YOUR ANALYST:

Where do I need to turn learning into experience?

What is the "big picture" in this situation, and how do these parts fit into that picture?

ANCESTOR

Tone

You prefer to see past, present, and future possibilities for others' lives, as well as for your own.

You can "see" all of the lines of heritage both on a Soulful level and on a physical level. You have an understanding of what can be released in order to be free of the ancestral hold on a situation.

INFLUENTIAL WORDS:

Heritage

Past

Lineage

ABILITIES AND TALENTS:

You are able to help yourself and others rewrite the past

You have an ability to help yourself and others release ancestral holds on situations

CONSCIOUSLY EXPERIENCING THIS LANGUAGE:

Accepting your past

Being in balance and living in the present

Understanding the intertwining of past, present, and future

Appropriately focusing on the future

Being aware that miracles are created in the present

Unconsciously experiencing this Language:

Being stuck in your past

Living for the future

Being inflexible and full of judgment

Being weighed down by ancestral beliefs, programming, or rituals

Signs you are on the path:

You have accepted your past

You have released (and continue to release) ancestral patterns

Language Orientation:

The *Ancestor* is Action/Still. Before taking action, it is important that you tune in and reflect to understand what the next Divinely inspired action is.

Accessing and Attracting Support:

Mentor (Axiom of Quest) – These individuals provide guidance and mentoring. They can help the *Ancestor* mentor the love inside of them to release the past.

Monk (Axiom of Translation) – These individuals understand the beauty of life and access stillness to feel and be more in tune with that beauty. They can help the *Ancestors* feel the peace and beauty of their lives.

Connoisseur (Tone) – These individuals understand how to accept themselves and others. They can help the *Ancestor* accept themselves and their life.

IF YOUR BUSINESS'S TONE IS ANCESTOR:

You understand the company's mission

You understand the company's past, present, and future, and do not get weighed down by past "mistakes"

You have incorporated flexibility into the company systems, while maintaining its structure and purpose

A CHILD WHO SPEAKS THIS LANGUAGE WILL THRIVE IN AN ENVIRONMENT THAT:

Provides them with an understanding of where they come from and where they are going

Provides them with flexible structure

Provides them with an appropriate focus on being in the present

QUESTIONS TO ASK YOUR ANCESTOR:

Where can I let go of something from my past?

What family pattern can I release?

Ark Builder

Tone

You prefer to go through life as a master architect, seeing the big, grand structures for creation. You see the simple construction of intricate structures and understand that creation is a learning process.

Influential words:

Form

Innovative

Assemble

Abilities and talents:

You are able to see the completed ark, and all of its individual boards, all at the same time

You are able to see a totally different way of utilizing the "how" of the world

Consciously experiencing this Language:

Recognizing different strategies and being able to communicate them to others

Accepting your leadership role as the "architect" of situations

Co-creating with the Universe (the master architect) to build something new

Not feeling the need to participate in all of the "doing" in your creations

Enlisting the nurturing support of others to assist in the "doing"

Unconsciously experiencing this Language:

Setting yourself apart because you feel misunderstood

Feeling as if no one else shares your vision

Struggling to communicate your vision in a clear way for others to be inspired

Feeling unsupported, as if there is no one to sustain you or to carry on the "how" of a project

Signs you are on the path:

You know what grand structures you wish to create for yourself

You create sustainable supportive relationships

You communicate clearly

Language Orientation:

The *Ark Builder* is Still. Your Soul has a desire to reflect. This reflection can help you see and understand the grand structure you wish to create or help others to create.

Accessing and Attracting Support:

Prophet (Axiom of Quest) – The *Prophet's* mission is to understand the message and to know how to deliver that message. They can help the *Ark Builder* with the "how" of their life.

Huntress/Hunter (Axiom of Translation) – These individuals are able to track and pursue what is being sought. They can help the *Ark Builder* receive resources.

Diplomat (Tone) – These individuals prefer to create relationships based on the foundation of love. They can help the *Ark Builder* create sustainable relationships.

IF YOUR BUSINESS'S TONE IS ARK BUILDER:

You are clearly communicating to your audience what you offer

You have support teams in place to take care of the "doing"

You clearly define your leadership role in your community, with your clients and within the industry

A CHILD WHO SPEAKS THIS LANGUAGE WILL THRIVE IN AN ENVIRONMENT THAT:

Provides them with opportunities to lead

Provides them with opportunities to share their big vision of things

Provides them opportunities to act and bring others together to see the manifestation of their big ideas

QUESTIONS TO ASK YOUR ARK BUILDER:

How can I be innovative in this situation?

What do I get to let go of in order to communicate more clearly?

Artisan

Tone

You prefer to go through life honing your skills and utilizing them to create something that is useful or tangible in the world.

You also provide others with opportunities to develop crafts, skills, and/or talents that benefit their lives in a tangible way.

INFLUENTIAL WORDS:

Talent

Dexterity

Physical

ABILITIES AND TALENTS:

You are a master craftsman

You share your many skills and talents with others

CONSCIOUSLY EXPERIENCING THIS LANGUAGE:

Incorporating new skills and abilities into your life without fear or attachment

Incorporating Divine energy into your creations

Having a healthy respect for your creations and your talents

Applying your talents for creations that improve your physical world

Unconsciously experiencing this Language:

Judging yourself for not focusing on just one skill or talent

Judging yourself or others for not incorporating new skills "quickly enough"

Feeling deprived, as if you don't have the resources you need to create

Being out of balance between the spiritual and physical planes

Being a perfectionist

Signs you are on the path:

You know how you wish to apply your gifts and talents to change your life and the lives of others

You have a process to connect to the Divine within you

Language Orientation:

The *Artisan* is Action. Your Soul has a desire to move directly into action. This can create the experience of "doing" all the time without receiving. Simply pausing will open you more up to receiving.

Accessing and Attracting Support:

Politician (Axiom of Quest) – These individuals provide others with the forum to speak their truth. They can help the *Artisan* speak the truth about their gifts and talents.

Purveyor (Axiom of Translation) – These individuals have access to an unlimited supply of resources. They can help the *Artisan* receive resources to help with their creations.

Disillusionist (Tone) – These individuals break down illusions to create a more sustaining life. They can help the *Artisan* create a more beneficial belief structure.

IF YOUR BUSINESS'S TONE IS ARTISAN:

You continually update the company's talents

You allow the proper "time" between creation and distribution

You have clear policies in place for compensation

A CHILD WHO SPEAKS THIS LANGUAGE WILL THRIVE IN AN ENVIRONMENT THAT:

Provides them with opportunities to explore their talents and gifts

Encourages patience

Provides them with a healthy understanding that it is acceptable to make "mistakes"

QUESTIONS TO ASK YOUR ARTISAN:

What skill or talent am I mastering in this situation?

How will my creation impact the physical world?

BEEKEEPER

Tone

You prefer to go through life being the "keeper" of productivity (mental, spiritual, or physical).

INFLUENTIAL WORDS:

Productivity

Focus

Direction

ABILITIES AND TALENTS:

You are able to communicate effectively and teach this skill to others

You are able to understand and teach others how to concentrate more fully and work more harmoniously together

CONSCIOUSLY EXPERIENCING THIS LANGUAGE:

Knowing what steps to take to increase your own productivity with ease

Being without attachment to your suggestions to others

Empowering yourself with agility and Divine inspiration

Empowering yourself and others without judgment or inhibition

Understanding how being still adds to a productive life

Taking chances to build new skills that highlight yourself and others

Unconsciously experiencing this Language:

Forgetting to enjoy the fruits of your labor

Judging your own productivity, or another's

Being a workaholic

Not seeing or appreciating your own contributions, or others'

Being a perfectionist

Fearing the stillness

Being afraid to take chances or experience new situations

Signs you are on the path:

You know what you would like to create with your skills and gifts

You are without judgment for your own productivity levels, and others

Language Orientation:

The *Beekeeper* is Action/Still. Your Soul has a desire to reflect prior to taking action. This pause to reflect will allow the *Beekeeper* to understand all the complexities of a situation.

Accessing and Attracting Support:

Mentor (Axiom of Quest) – The *Mentor's* mission is to guide. They can help the *Beekeeper* understand what they need to create a balanced life.

Huntress/Hunter (Axiom of Translation) – These individuals will be known here for how they track what they are seeking. They can help the *Beekeeper* understand when to pause and when to pursue.

Collaborator (Tone) – These individuals prefer to collaborate with others. They can help the *Beekeeper* to work better in groups.

IF YOUR BUSINESS'S TONE IS BEEKEEPER:

You have systems in place to support productivity

You provide opportunities for yourself and others to develop skills and talents

You have clearly defined hours of operation and stick to them for balance

A CHILD WHO SPEAKS THIS LANGUAGE WILL THRIVE IN AN ENVIRONMENT THAT:

Provides them with opportunities to explore new skills and talents

Provides them with a balance of work and play

Provides them with the foundations for working within a team

QUESTIONS TO ASK YOUR BEEKEEPER:

Where am I judging my own productivity in this situation?

How can I enjoy the fruits of my labor?

Bodybuilder

Tone

You prefer to focus on the internal construction of things.

You are able to build form by working with nature to enhance it physically, to amend or add to it with the Soul's help and guidance.

When a structure is reinforced then it is able to support more weight. That means more of the Soul can be incorporated into that structure.

INFLUENTIAL WORDS:

Configuration

Internal

Essence

ABILITIES AND TALENTS:

You are able to enhance form from the inside out, using the Soul to support an individual's natural form

You are able to help yourself and others release pain

CONSCIOUSLY EXPERIENCING THIS LANGUAGE:

Being able to perceive how all the building blocks of form and Soul fit together

Recognizing where building more support is required

Letting go of pain and judgment

UNCONSCIOUSLY EXPERIENCING THIS LANGUAGE:

Focusing only on building one aspect of structure, creating imbalance

Holding onto pain, which weakens your structure

Not feeling connected to your body or spirit

SIGNS YOU ARE ON THE PATH:

You know what part of your own structure you wish to enhance

You are releasing your own pain

LANGUAGE ORIENTATION:

The *Bodybuilder* is Action/Still. Your Soul has a desire to reflect prior to moving into action. This allows you to connect with Divine guidance and determine what part of your structure you wish to enhance.

ACCESSING AND ATTRACTING SUPPORT:

Politician (Axiom of Quest) – These individuals provide others with the forum to speak their truth. They can help the *Bodybuilder* be honest with themselves and others.

Monk (Axiom of Translation) – These individuals are all about stillness. They can help the *Bodybuilder* to listen within.

Disillusionist (Tone) – These individuals break down illusions to create more sustainable ones. They can help the *Bodybuilder* create safety within their own body.

IF YOUR BUSINESS'S TONE IS BODYBUILDER:

You understand what structures you are enhancing for others

You create systems for the business to build and improve its structure on a regular basis

You are clear with your clients what "enhancements" you are offering them and why

A CHILD WHO SPEAKS THIS LANGUAGE WILL THRIVE IN AN ENVIRONMENT THAT:

Provides them with an understanding of how their body works

Provides them with a structure to listen to their body

Supports them in expressing love, honesty, and compassion for their own choices

QUESTIONS TO ASK YOUR BODYBUILDER:

What part of my own form do I wish to enhance?

How can I use my spirit to enhance my form?

BOXER

Tone

Your Soulful personality is about force and movement. You are able to think and react quickly, especially during confrontational situations.

Innately, you understand when to confront a situation head-on and when to sidestep. Your nature is that of a powerhouse.

INFLUENTIAL WORDS:

Movement

Lightness

Focus

ABILITIES AND TALENTS:

You are able to make decisions that are for the greatest good of all during stressful situations

You are a good strategist and have inexhaustible courage and strength

CONSCIOUSLY EXPERIENCING THIS LANGUAGE:

Accepting your ability to assess a situation and make quick decisions gracefully

Trusting yourself and your intuition

Operating with the intention of the greatest good of all

Understanding when to sidestep and when to confront things (internally and externally)

Tapping into the courage and strength within you

Understanding that there is no such thing as "failure"

Understanding and keeping your own rules of conduct

Understanding that sidestepping confrontation is not a sign of weakness

Trusting that you will be supported in moving beyond your comfort zone

UNCONSCIOUSLY EXPERIENCING THIS LANGUAGE:

Experiencing constant drama and confrontation

Repeating the same situations over and over again to prove that you are strong and courageous

Being afraid of confrontation, avoiding it at all costs

Being in judgment of yourself and others

Bullying yourself and others

SIGNS YOU ARE ON THE PATH:

You trust yourself completely

You are operating with the intention of the greatest good of all

You know your rules of conduct and live by them

LANGUAGE ORIENTATION:

The *Boxer* is Action/Still. Your Soul has a desire to create balance between reflection and action. It is important that you listen to the guidance inside, which will allow you to know whether to sidestep or confront a situation.

ACCESSING AND ATTRACTING SUPPORT:

Prophet (Axiom of Quest) – These individuals not only know the message, they also know the structure needed to deliver that message. They can help the *Boxer* be unafraid to confront and hear messages from their own Soul.

Sun (Axiom of Translation) – These individuals are always rising to enlightenment. They can help the *Boxer* feel their connection with the Divine.

Intellect (Tone) – These individuals prefer to utilize their mind. They can help the *Boxer* communicate effectively.

IF YOUR BUSINESS'S TONE IS BOXER:

You know what you are offering others the opportunity to confront

You set attainable goals for the company, and you create systems to assess those goals and see how each project is a success in its own way

You have clear structures to communicate the rules of conduct within the company

A CHILD WHO SPEAKS THIS LANGUAGE WILL THRIVE IN AN ENVIRONMENT THAT:

Provides them with an understanding of when it is appropriate to "fight" and when to "walk away"

Supports them with learning to trust their intuition

Provides them with a nurturing and supportive system of values

QUESTIONS TO ASK YOUR BOXER:

Where can I trust my guidance in this situation?

What do I get to confront within myself in this situation?

BRICKLAYER

Tone

You prefer to go through life recognizing how "patterns" are laid out, aware of how those patterns can be rearranged or reapplied for a better existence.

INFLUENTIAL WORDS:

Pattern

Assemble

Foundation

ABILITIES AND TALENTS:

You are able to see and create patterns

You understand how patterns can be applied to nurture and sustain life

CONSCIOUSLY EXPERIENCING THIS LANGUAGE:

Understanding that sometimes you will design new patterns and at other times you will just follow a blueprint

Understanding how each pattern is laid out, and which "blocks" to move to create a more sustainable life

Understanding what patterns of your own get to be rearranged or recreated

Understanding that every pattern is based on the concepts of love and safety

Rearranging the patterns of your life without everything falling apart

Integrating into body, mind, and spirit the wisdom from patterns in your own life and others'

UNCONSCIOUSLY EXPERIENCING THIS LANGUAGE:

Feeling like you have to reinvent the wheel

Being unable to see the patterns that are right in front of you

Not understanding how the patterns you see fit into your own life

Using fear as a way to create walls or non-nurturing patterns

Ignoring your inner wisdom

Resisting the wisdom of your own patterns

SIGNS YOU ARE ON THE PATH:

You know what patterns need to be rearranged in your own life

You know what blocks in your patterns get to be removed

LANGUAGE ORIENTATION:

The *Bricklayer* is Action. Your Soul has a desire to move directly into action. It is important that you create inspired action or you will be creating patterns just for the sake of doing something.

ACCESSING AND ATTRACTING SUPPORT:

Pioneer (Axiom of Quest) – These individuals help others forge new roads. They can help the *Bricklayer* break through their own patterns.

Monk (Axiom of Translation) – These individuals are all about the stillness. They can help the *Bricklayer* go within for the answers.

Escalator (Tone) – These individuals are about rising to enlightenment at a steady pace. They can help the *Bricklayer* understand where they would like to go and what pace to set.

IF YOUR BUSINESS'S TONE IS BRICKLAYER:

You are clear about your customer base and the pattern you are helping others to utilize

You communicate clearly when the company's patterns are updated

You understand how the patterns you see with your customers apply to the company

A CHILD WHO SPEAKS THIS LANGUAGE WILL THRIVE IN AN ENVIRONMENT THAT:

Provides them with an understanding of how things "fit together"

Provides them with an understanding of how to express the patterns they see in an appropriate way

Provides them with the skills to understand their intuition and inner wisdom

QUESTIONS TO ASK YOUR BRICKLAYER:

What pattern in my life is not serving me?

Where in this situation am I trying to reinvent the wheel?

CAPITALIST

Tone

You are skilled at making use of any form of prosperity, abundance of any kind, to produce more prosperity. You innately understand what needs to be exchanged for all parties to achieve prosperity. It is important for the *Capitalist* to remember that we all come with our own capital within us.

INFLUENTIAL WORDS:

Abundance

Balance

Compensation

ABILITIES AND TALENTS:

You are able to understand how to generate abundance

You have a keen ability to understand the balance of giving and receiving

CONSCIOUSLY EXPERIENCING THIS LANGUAGE:

Manifesting abundance or a profusion of anything you desire with balance and harmony

Understanding the energy of abundance and prosperity

Understanding that we have a Divine right to be abundant, and that it is a choice to live otherwise

Understanding true, balanced compensation

Being grateful for your abundant life

UNCONSCIOUSLY EXPERIENCING THIS LANGUAGE:

Feeling blocked, choosing to live without abundance

Taking unnecessary risks that produce undesired outcomes

Believing that there are inherent risks or penalties in achieving prosperity

Feeling as if there is not enough

SIGNS YOU ARE ON THE PATH:

You know your own value and are open to receiving

You know that there is enough pie for everyone, and all you have to do is ask for your slice

You are balanced in giving and receiving

LANGUAGE ORIENTATION:

The *Capitalist* is Action. Your Soul has a desire to move directly into action. Remember that too much action can result in not being still enough to receive.

ACCESSING AND ATTRACTING SUPPORT:

Caretaker (Axiom of Quest) – These individuals are custodians of a belief, theory, object, etc. They can help the *Capitalist* hold this belief of abundance with compassion and love.

Heart Conscious (Axiom of Translation) – These individuals experience the world through the heart. They can help the *Capitalist* understand the spirit of compensation.

Bricklayer (Tone) – These individuals understand how to create new patterns. They can help the *Capitalist* let go of limiting patterns regarding money, abundance, and compensation.

IF YOUR BUSINESS'S TONE IS CAPITALIST:

You know the value of the company and you express it clearly

You are clear about what you are providing and the structure for compensation

You know that there is enough of everything for everyone

A CHILD WHO SPEAKS THIS LANGUAGE WILL THRIVE IN AN ENVIRONMENT THAT:

Provides them with a healthy understanding of money

Provides them with a deep sense of their own value

Provides them with healthy boundaries so they can express their value

QUESTIONS TO ASK YOUR CAPITALIST:

How am I limiting my value?

How can I open up my receiving?

CAPTAIN

Tone

You prefer to be the head of an influential group, to be in charge. As the superintendent of this group, you are the acting authority to ensure that the policies and regulations are enforced.

Each member of this group, including the *Captain*, is acting to complete a common task, goal, or mission. You do not feel satisfied with any other position and will work toward achieving the highest rank in your area of expertise.

INFLUENTIAL WORDS:

Leader

Power

Destiny

ABILITIES AND TALENTS:

You are able to understand what systems and procedures to provide that will produce the best results

You have a deep level of courage and compassion

You know when to seek advice and when to go with your gut

CONSCIOUSLY EXPERIENCING THIS LANGUAGE:

Commanding your group and yourself with an even hand

Providing motivation for the group and yourself

Knowing the procedures and strategies that will produce the best results (with the intention of the greatest good of all)

Soliciting, through goodwill and Divine guidance, the support of resources and people to assist with the completion of the common task, goal, or mission and to support your rise to power

Accepting your power and utilizing it with Divine guidance

Having compassion for yourself and others

Understanding when to seek advice, when to accept advice, and when to look within for guidance

Understanding how the talents of each group member add to the power of the group and its talents

Having the respect of your group

UNCONSCIOUSLY EXPERIENCING THIS LANGUAGE:

Expressing impatience for and intolerance of yourself or others

Living in fear about making decisions

Being a perfectionist, demanding impossible standards for yourself or others

Being unable to find a group to lead or being removed (figuratively or literally) from your group

Using any means to obtain the top position of power, with little attention to the consequences of your actions

Trying to control everything, living in fear of losing control

Fearing what others think, trying to people-please in order to receive respect

SIGNS YOU ARE ON THE PATH:

You are comfortable asking for and receiving assistance

You are well grounded and balanced, leading with an even hand

LANGUAGE ORIENTATION:

The *Captain* is Action. Your Soul has a desire to move directly into action. It is important that you check in prior to taking action to gain guidance from within and from others around you.

ACCESSING AND ATTRACTING SUPPORT:

Equalizer (Axiom of Quest) – The *Equalizer's* mission is to create a balanced formula for internal sustainability. They can help the *Captain* achieve balance, allowing them to lead with an even hand.

Image Maker (Axiom of Translation) – These individuals see the essence of a being and then help bring that essence into reality. They can help the *Captain* "see" the essence of an individual and therefore understand them better.

Chieftain (Tone) – These individuals are born leaders who people automatically turn to in order to be led. They can help the *Captain* understand how to earn and hold respect.

IF YOUR BUSINESS'S TONE IS CAPTAIN:

You are clear about your goals, tasks, and mission, so success can be monitored and attained

You are clear about what resources you need to receive and have systems in place to obtain them

You are clear about the talents and gifts of each member of the company, and you have systems in place to support and acknowledge them

A CHILD WHO SPEAKS THIS LANGUAGE WILL THRIVE IN AN ENVIRONMENT THAT:

Provides them with a deep sense of self and compassion

Provides them with the ability to lead others through motivation and love, not fear

Provides them with the safety to ask for and receive assistance

QUESTIONS TO ASK YOUR CAPTAIN:

What do I get to let go of in order to be a better leader?

Where am I not tolerant or compassionate towards myself or others?

CARTER

Tone

You have one single message that you relay to yourself and others. Every fiber of your being is encoded with this message. For example, if your message is "love," everything you feel, speak, and do is about illustrating the message of love.

INFLUENTIAL WORDS:

Message

Listen

Love

ABILITIES AND TALENTS:

You are able to provide your message to everyone, in just the way they need to hear it (if they choose to listen)

You are able to understand the heart of a situation

CONSCIOUSLY EXPERIENCING THIS LANGUAGE:

Knowing and hearing your own message

Knowing that everything you do, say, think, and feel is coded with this message, and that there are no limits to expressing it

Releasing attachment to individuals taking action on that message

UNCONSCIOUSLY EXPERIENCING THIS LANGUAGE:

Being unclear about your message, or judging it

Feeling lost because you are not hearing your message

Limiting your message

Being attached to how others utilize the message

SIGNS YOU ARE ON THE PATH:

You have a structure in place to support you in being still.

You take time for yourself and your own growth

You have let go of attachment to how the message is received

LANGUAGE ORIENTATION:

The *Carter* is Action. Your Soul has a desire to take action. You need to set aside time to be still in order to create inspired action and hear your own message.

ACCESSING AND ATTRACTING SUPPORT:

Observer (Axiom of Quest) – The *Observer's* mission is to observe, record, and report. They can help the *Carter* understand how their message has been displayed, interpreted, and received throughout history. This will help them release judgment.

Strategist (Axiom of Translation) – These individuals can help the *Carter* step up strategies and systems for their message.

Developer (Tone) – These individuals are investors. They can help the *Carter* in how to grow and advance their message.

IF YOUR BUSINESS'S TONE IS CARTER:

You know and follow the message of the business

You set appropriate boundaries for the business

You release attachment to how the message is received

A CHILD WHO SPEAKS THIS LANGUAGE WILL THRIVE IN AN ENVIRONMENT THAT:

Provides them with tools to hear and express their message

Provides them with the tools not to take life too personally

Provides them with opportunities to feel safe

QUESTIONS TO ASK YOUR CARTER:

Where am I moving so fast that I'm unable or unwilling to hear my message?

What part of my life can I bring more of my message to?

CHIEFTAIN

Tone

You are a leader of groups of people that share a common awareness, principle, or belief. This group or series of groups might appear small, and yet they can have a huge impact. *Chieftains* are individuals that other people easily place their trust in to lead with a particular focus or goal.

INFLUENTIAL WORDS:

Listen

Honest

Leading

ABILITIES AND TALENTS:

You have a keen sense of knowing the answer

You understand the difference between your voice, the community's voice, and Divine voice

CONSCIOUSLY EXPERIENCING THIS LANGUAGE:

Accepting your leadership role

Knowing you are not responsible for the individual actions of group members

Making choices based on Divine inspiration

Allowing others to speak their mind and truth prior to making a choice for the community or group

Understanding the difference between your voice, the voice of the community, and Divine voice

Being balanced in giving and receiving

UNCONSCIOUSLY EXPERIENCING THIS LANGUAGE:

Leading by control

Ruling yourself or others by fear

Insisting on your way or the highway

Judging your community, feeling unsupported by it

Giving or taking too much

Living in doubt

Rejecting your leadership role

SIGNS YOU ARE ON THE PATH:

You have accepted your leadership role

You feel loved and supported by the Universe

LANGUAGE ORIENTATION:

The *Chieftain* is Action. Your Soul has a desire to act first and reflect later. It is important for the *Chieftain* to take Divinely inspired action and not get caught up in doing for the sake of doing.

ACCESSING AND ATTRACTING SUPPORT:

Counselor (Axiom of Quest) – These individuals share guidance in a particular area and can help the *Chieftain* bring that knowledge to the group.

Pleasure Seeker (Axiom of Translation) – These individuals can teach the *Chieftain* how to have fun and not be serious all the time.

Closer (Tone) – These individuals can teach the *Chieftain* how to understand the details that will help bring forth conclusions, both for the *Chieftain* and the group.

Also see the *Guardian* (Tone), page 363.

IF YOUR BUSINESS'S TONE IS CHIEFTAIN:

You have clear and open channels of communication

You know the leadership role of the business

You make choices for the company based on Divine guidance and intuition, not out of fear

A CHILD WHO SPEAKS THIS LANGUAGE WILL THRIVE IN AN ENVIRONMENT THAT:

Provides them with the tools to lead by example

Provides them with the ability to take responsibility for their own actions

Provides them the opportunity to speak their truth in an appropriate way

QUESTIONS TO ASK YOUR CHIEFTAIN:

Where am I trying to force my leadership?

Where am I not accepting my role as chief?

CLOSER

Tone

You prefer to go through life guiding situations to completion. You receive details, through your own observations and the observations of others as well as through Divine Intelligence, and use these to bring closure, completion, or wholeness to situations.

Your extreme attentiveness to details and accuracy helps you bring forth conclusions. You notice details that others might not think are important, and this allows you to "close" a situation. You work well with others and are able to rely on your own intuition, skill, and observations to bring a situation to completion. You are able to collaborate and also rely on your own skill.

INFLUENTIAL WORDS:

Complete

Elements

Whole

CONSCIOUSLY EXPERIENCING THIS LANGUAGE:

Knowing when an assignment, project, job, relationship, etc. has served its usefulness in your life and on your journey

Letting go of things without judgment or regret

Knowing that no matter what you are complete inside

Not having attachment to situations you are guiding to completion

ABILITIES AND TALENTS:

You have an ability to catch details that others do not see or understand

You have an astute awareness of what can happen for situations to be complete

UNCONSCIOUSLY EXPERIENCING THIS LANGUAGE:

Seeing all of the details but not knowing how they fit together to create the big picture

Feeling incomplete

Having trouble creating conclusions

Keeping your knowledge hidden from yourself and others

SIGNS YOU ARE ON THE PATH:

You know when things in your life have run their course and can be let go of

You understand and feel your own completeness

You know what areas of your life feel incomplete and you are creating completion

LANGUAGE ORIENTATION:

The *Closer* is Action/Still. Your Soul has a desire to reflect prior to moving into action. This reflection will allow you to understand the details that others miss in order to help you close a situation.

ACCESSING AND ATTRACTING SUPPORT:

Negotiator (Axiom of Quest) – These individuals can teach the *Closer* how to close successful new deals for themselves and others.

Nurturer (Axiom of Translation) – These individuals can help the *Closer* understand what nurtures themselves and others. This will allow them to "see" more details.

Driver (Tone) – These individuals are amazing at creating focused movement. They can help the *Closer* understand when they are "pushing" too hard and when they get to let the natural momentum take over.

IF YOUR BUSINESS'S TONE IS CLOSER:

You understand both the details and the big picture

You are clear about what you are trying to close

You know what you are guiding others to close

A CHILD WHO SPEAKS THIS LANGUAGE WILL THRIVE IN AN ENVIRONMENT THAT:

Provides them with an understanding of when it is for the greatest good of all to let something go

Provides them with a strong sense of self-love so they do not judge themselves or others

Provides them with an understanding of what completes their life

QUESTIONS TO ASK YOUR CLOSER:

What detail am I not seeing or understanding that will help guide this situation to a natural conclusion?

Where do I feel incomplete in my life?

COLLABORATOR

Tone

You prefer to associate with others in an endeavor, activity, or common sphere of interest in order to bring forth a new or improved idea, thought, product, belief, relationship, solution, strategy, etc.

INFLUENTIAL WORDS:

Teamwork

Relationship

Co-create

ABILITIES AND TALENTS:

You are able to attract the finest people in their field to generate a new or comprehensive program, strategy, or solution

You invite and welcome into your life all kinds of individuals

CONSCIOUSLY EXPERIENCING THIS LANGUAGE:

Offering your own part of the collaboration and allowing others to step up as well

Bringing together amazing people and feeling confident and secure about your own talents and worth

Supporting and nurturing your own life through your collaborations

Having appropriate boundaries with your fellow collaborators

Being clear about your expectations

Co-creating with yourself and the Universe

UNCONSCIOUSLY EXPERIENCING THIS LANGUAGE:

Choosing to work independently out of fear

Withholding your input out of fear

Feeling separate and unsupported

Choosing inappropriate groups and creating co-dependent relationships

SIGNS YOU ARE ON THE PATH:

You know what true collaboration means to you and you communicate it to others

You create supportive relationships

LANGUAGE ORIENTATION:

The *Collaborator* is Action/Still. Your Soul has a desire to reflect prior to taking action. It is important that you allow yourself time for reflection so you can determine if this is a true collaboration that meets your Soul's desire.

ACCESSING AND ATTRACTING SUPPORT:

Politician (Axiom of Quest) – These individuals provide others with the forum to speak their truth. They can help the *Collaborator* feel secure voicing their needs and desires.

Sextant (Axiom of Translation) – These individuals are able to see where people are on their journey. They can help the *Collaborator* see the next step on their journey.

Conductor (Tone) – These individuals understand what brings out the best in others. They can help the *Collaborator* understand the individual role of each member in the group.

IF YOUR BUSINESS'S TONE IS COLLABORATOR:

You have firm structures and guidelines in place for your collaborations

You understand the company's role in any collaboration

You create strategic check-ins to determine whether collaborations are on target with the company's mission and purpose

A CHILD WHO SPEAKS THIS LANGUAGE WILL THRIVE IN AN ENVIRONMENT THAT:

Provides them with good communication skills

Provides them with the chance to collaborate with you as a parent

Provides them with a foundation for accepting others for their unique gifts

QUESTIONS TO ASK YOUR COLLABORATOR:

What fears does collaboration bring up and why?

What do I get to let go of or allow in order to be a "better" collaborator?

Conductor

Tone

You are a born leader, a guide or manager by nature.

You can be highly organized and effective. When you step into your power you can utilize Divine energy to guide situations for the highest good of all.

Influential words:

Guide

Lead

Highlight

Abilities and talents:

You are able to see the talents and gifts of others and bring them out into the light

You lead with a velvet hand through grace

Consciously experiencing this Language:

Understanding the importance of having a group or community

Understanding that you are an important part of this group or community

Knowing how to highlight and bring out the best in each group member, including yourself

Accepting your leadership abilities

Joyfully connecting with others without moving into servitude

UNCONSCIOUSLY EXPERIENCING THIS LANGUAGE:

Trying to control a situation so you are directing, rather than highlighting yourself and others

Being over-critical and judging yourself or others

Over-emphasizing others

Acting out of servitude rather than joyful service

Feeling exhausted from leading others

People-pleasing

SIGNS YOU ARE ON THE PATH:

You know your values and talents

You know and feel comfortable in your community

You lead with love and grace

LANGUAGE ORIENTATION:

The *Conductor* is Action/Still. Your Soul has a desire to reflect prior to taking action. It is important that you allow yourself the space to feel, understand, and express your gifts and talents.

ACCESSING AND ATTRACTING SUPPORT:

Bridgewalker (Axiom of Quest) – These individuals have an innate knowing of how to create and form bridges of spiritual, mental, material, and emotional support. They can help the *Conductor* create bridges for their community members.

Image Maker (Axiom of Translation) – These individuals can help the *Conductor* understand how to "see" more of an individual's Soul in order to highlight it in the community.

Diplomat (Tone) – These individuals can help the *Conductor* understand how to establish and strengthen new relationships. This will help build a community.

IF YOUR BUSINESS'S TONE IS CONDUCTOR:

You need to know the talents and gifts of your business and not be afraid to highlight them

You need to focus on highlighting your community members at the same time as the business

You can stress the leadership qualities of the business

A CHILD WHO SPEAKS THIS LANGUAGE WILL THRIVE IN AN ENVIRONMENT THAT:

Provides them with an understanding of their gifts and talents

Encourages their natural leadership abilities

Provides them with tools for trust so they don't try to control situations

QUESTIONS TO ASK YOUR CONDUCTOR:

Where can I highlight one of my gifts and talents?

How can I step more into my Soulful leadership abilities?

CONNOISSEUR

Tone

You have the competence to provide astute conclusions in a particular subject or in several subjects.

You have an innate knowing of what is going to "sell," be accepted, or resonate for yourself and others. You are able to see what has been created with heart and Soul.

INFLUENTIAL WORDS:

Accepted

Astute

Resonate

ABILITIES AND TALENTS:

You are able to see what has been created with heart and Soul

You have a keen awareness of what is going to "sell" or be accepted

CONSCIOUSLY EXPERIENCING THIS LANGUAGE:

Accepting yourself

Creating a life full of acceptance

Releasing attachment to your conclusions

Seeing the many layers of something and knowing what "went into it" to create it

Creating without judgment

UNCONSCIOUSLY EXPERIENCING THIS LANGUAGE:

Experiencing control issues, wanting it to be "your way or the highway"

Feeling like you do not know what is accepted or what will "sell" for yourself

Not accepting yourself

SIGNS YOU ARE ON THE PATH:

You know what you wish to create, knowing and trusting that it will be accepted by others

You understand and convey to others in a non-judgmental manner both what is being accepted and what needs to be accepted

LANGUAGE ORIENTATION:

The *Connoisseur* is Action. Your Soul has a desire to move directly into action. This comes from an innate knowing of what needs to happen for acceptance. Too much action may cause you to move into non-acceptance.

ACCESSING AND ATTRACTING SUPPORT:

Genius (Axiom of Quest) – These individuals usher in a new way of existence that will influence and change history. They can help the *Connoisseur* understand how this new way of thinking and feeling will impact the way something is accepted.

Heart Conscious (Axiom of Translation) – These individuals experience the world through the heart. They can help the *Connoisseur* understand heart and Spirit in a more profound way.

Ark Builder (Tone) – These individuals have a unique perspective in influencing the "how" of things. They can help the *Connoisseur* understand pathways to explain, express, and bring to others what has been created with heart and Soul.

IF YOUR BUSINESS'S TONE IS CONNOISSEUR:

You need to know what product or service you are offering to the world and trust that it will be accepted

You understand how to convey to others your special talents in understanding and creating acceptance

You are clear about the value of what you bring to the table

A CHILD WHO SPEAKS THIS LANGUAGE WILL THRIVE IN AN ENVIRONMENT THAT:

Lets them know that they are valued, supported, and accepted

Provides them with the communication skills to explain how others can create and move into acceptance

Provides them with the knowledge of what it feels like to be operating from the heart

QUESTIONS TO ASK YOUR CONNOISSEUR:

Where do I get to accept more of myself?

What do I want to create that is filled with heart and Soul and will be accepted?

DELIBERATOR

Tone

You are slow and steady. You are leisurely and steady in movement or action. You can appear to be unhurried and will move in action after all of the pros and cons are weighed and you believe a balance has been met.

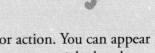

INFLUENTIAL WORDS:

Balance

Intentional

Conscious

ABILITIES AND TALENTS:

You are able to understand all of the pros and cons of a decision

You are able to understand innately what direction to take

CONSCIOUSLY EXPERIENCING THIS LANGUAGE:

Weighing both the mind and spirit in decisions

Creating balance for yourself and others

Having the courage to act

Understanding the intention of your deliberation

Deliberating without attachment

UNCONSCIOUSLY EXPERIENCING THIS LANGUAGE:

Feeling overwhelmed by balancing the pros and cons of a decision, getting stuck in the deliberation process

Finding it difficult to create movement and progress

Being afraid to make a decision

Making decisions based only on either the mind or emotion

SIGNS YOU ARE ON THE PATH:

You are balanced in your deliberations

You base your decisions on both mind and spirit

You are not afraid to act

LANGUAGE ORIENTATION:

The *Deliberator* is Action/Still. Your Soul has a desire to reflect before moving into action. Balance is important so you don't move into action for the sake of action or get stuck in the stillness.

ACCESSING AND ATTRACTING SUPPORT:

Negotiator (Axiom of Quest) – These individuals can help the *Deliberator* understand how to create deals that support the greatest good of all. This will help them understand where and how to act.

Motivator (Axiom of Translation) – These individuals can teach the *Deliberator* to understand what is motivating their decision-making process.

Collaborator (Tone) – These individuals can help the *Deliberator* understand when to co-create with themselves so the decision-making process is more fluid and graceful.

IF YOUR BUSINESS'S TONE IS DELIBERATOR:

You know when action can be taken

You have structures for decision-making processes

You know which decisions can be acted on right away and which decisions need to be weighed

A CHILD WHO SPEAKS THIS LANGUAGE WILL THRIVE IN AN ENVIRONMENT THAT:

Provides them with a structure to know when to move into action

Provides them with an understanding of when to go with their gut

Provides them with an understanding of how they make decisions

QUESTIONS TO ASK YOUR DELIBERATOR:

Am I getting weighed down by the decision-making process?

What am I afraid of that is preventing me from feeling and understanding my decision?

DEVELOPER

Tone

You prefer to live by investing in life and in your Soul. This means making investments in the growth and advancement of yourself, others, and the world. These investments can be in the form of goods, services, relationships, etc.

You are always asking, "What will it take for this to be expanded?"

INFLUENTIAL WORDS:

Invest

Advancement

Growth

ABILITIES AND TALENTS:

You are able to see what it takes for growth to occur, and to find resources to fuel that growth

You are able to see expansion in all areas of life

CONSCIOUSLY EXPERIENCING THIS LANGUAGE:

Understanding that not everything wants to be expanded or advanced, only directing your resources to those situations that desire development

Recognizing that permission is required before offering your investment in others

Knowing which investments will support your expansion

Working with the Universal good to create development and expansion for the greatest good of all

Knowing that there is no such thing as a "magic pill" for expansion; choosing wisely in your investments for development

UNCONSCIOUSLY EXPERIENCING THIS LANGUAGE:

Forcing an expansion or development

Looking for the magic pill

Investing resources in a situation that is not ready for expansion

Believing that the key to expansion is outside of you

Developing or expanding with no regard for the greater good

Investing your resources out of fear and doubt

SIGNS YOU ARE ON THE PATH:

You know what you require to develop your own life

You invest wisely in expansion

You do not force expansion

LANGUAGE ORIENTATION:

The *Developer* is Action. Your Soul has a desire to move directly into action. This can create an unbalanced expansion. It is suggested that you reflect on how to create balanced expansion for yourself, then offer that balance to others.

ACCESSING AND ATTRACTING SUPPORT:

Matriarch/Patriarch (Axiom of Quest) – The mission of a *Matriarch/Patriarch* is to lead a community. They can help the *Developer* expand their leadership qualities.

Huntress/Hunter (Axiom of Translation) – These individuals can track and find what they desire. They can help the *Developer* understand what direction to take in order to find what they are seeking.

Conductor (Tone) – These individuals prefer to bring out the best in others. They can help the *Developer* understand what needs to be highlighted within them to achieve their desires.

IF YOUR BUSINESS'S TONE IS DEVELOPER:

You understand what kinds of expansion the company is offering

You understand what investments the company is making and why

You have guidelines for your ideal client in order to avoid trying to drag someone into expanding

A CHILD WHO SPEAKS THIS LANGUAGE WILL THRIVE IN AN ENVIRONMENT THAT:

Provides them with an appropriate understanding of what they are investing in each situation

Provides them with ways to connect with others and determine what they truly desire

Provides them with an understanding of cause and effect

QUESTIONS TO ASK YOUR DEVELOPER:

How would I like to expand internally?

Will this investment be beneficial to my expansion, or am I investing out of fear?

DIONYSIAN

Tone

You internalize transformation through experiences.

You process things very quickly and are interested in feeling, seeing, and observing as much as you can while you are on this planet.

INFLUENTIAL WORDS:

Experience

Delight

Essence

ABILITIES AND TALENTS:

You are able to describe profound experiences in a way that supports others in opening up to experiencing it for themselves

You sort through information quickly in order to determine the benefits of an experience so you can fully enjoy it

CONSCIOUSLY EXPERIENCING THIS LANGUAGE:

Understanding that some experiences, like wine, need to be "drunk" a little more slowly in order to savor the taste

Learning through nurturing experiences

Finding pleasure in all experiences

Releasing attachment to the experiences you are offering others

Unconsciously experiencing this Language:

Being "addicted" to the delight of the physical plane as an avoidance strategy

Experiencing frenzy and chaos

Believing that pain is the only experience you can learn from

Feeling unsatisfied by any experience

Being afraid to experience anything new

Signs you are on the path:

You know what you wish to experience to support your life purpose

You offer experiences to others without attachment

Language Orientation:

The *Dionysian* is Action/Still. Your Soul has a desire to reflect prior to moving into action. This allows you to reflect on what the experience will bring you and whether it is in the greatest good to move forward in the situation.

Accessing and Attracting Support:

Pioneer (Axiom of Quest) – These individuals create new roads for themselves and others. They can help the *Dionysian* create new experiences.

Huntress/Hunter (Axiom of Translation) – These individuals know how to engage, explore, track, and secure what they are seeking. They can help the *Dionysian* understand what they are looking for in an experience.

Collaborator (Tone) – These individuals are interested in co-creating with others. They can help the *Dionysian* bring together different groups to experience new relationships.

IF YOUR BUSINESS'S TONE IS DIONYSIAN:

You understand what new experiences you are offering your audience

You do not promise your audience a particular response or any specific benefits of the experience you offer

You do not impose deadlines out of fear or the need to experience something new

A CHILD WHO SPEAKS THIS LANGUAGE WILL THRIVE IN AN ENVIRONMENT THAT:

Provides them with new experiences

Provides them with structured time for quiet

Provides them with a healthy experience of gratitude

QUESTIONS TO ASK YOUR DIONYSIAN:

What new experience do I wish to understand?

Where am I trying to move through an experience that calls for stillness?

DIPLOMAT

Tone

You prefer to generate new agreements by creating relationships of love for yourself and others. You help create these new "deals" by establishing, strengthening, and assisting in the formation of a new relationship or the deepening of an existing one.

You have a keen sense of what each individual needs in a situation in order for a true compromise to be met, for all parties to feel that something has been achieved, and for each party to feel as if they have "won."

INFLUENTIAL WORDS:

Cooperation

Love

Connection

ABILITIES AND TALENTS:

You are able to offer true compromises that create and deepen relationships

You are tactful and skillful in managing delicate situations

CONSCIOUSLY EXPERIENCING THIS LANGUAGE:

Being able to see all sides without attachment

Knowing what compromises can be made for each party

Creating new deals out of the consciousness of love

Knowing what new relationships you would like to create for yourself

Knowing what compromises you are making for yourself

Being respectful of others' free-will decisions

Having clear boundaries

Consciously connecting with yourself and others

UNCONSCIOUSLY EXPERIENCING THIS LANGUAGE:

Trying to people-please

Being over-critical and judgmental of yourself or others

Making sacrifices instead of compromises

Holding onto relationships that do not serve you, preventing yourself from creating new sustainable relationships

Creating co-dependent relationships

Closing yourself off from new relationships

Operating from a belief that love is conditional

SIGNS YOU ARE ON THE PATH:

You know what compromises (not sacrifices) you are making in relationships and in situations

You live without attachment

You show yourself love and create a deep relationship with yourself

LANGUAGE ORIENTATION:

The *Diplomat* is Action/Still. Your Soul has a desire to reflect prior to taking action. It is important that you allow yourself this time for reflection so you can understand all the sides of a situation and listen to Divine guidance.

ACCESSING AND ATTRACTING SUPPORT:

Mentor (Axiom of Quest) – The *Mentor's* mission is to guide themselves and others. They can teach the *Diplomat* to cultivate love within themselves.

Motivator (Axiom of Translation) – These individuals can show the *Diplomat* their true motivation in creating compromises and new relationships.

Firemaker (Tone) – These individuals ignite passion. They can help the *Diplomat* spark a fire within to move from people-pleasing to appropriate self-awareness.

IF YOUR BUSINESS'S TONE IS DIPLOMAT:

You have clear boundaries about what the company does and doesn't do

You have a system in place to make sure that the company doesn't sacrifice itself to make a deal

You have guidelines for creating relationships (e.g. joint ventures, partnerships, etc.)

A CHILD WHO SPEAKS THIS LANGUAGE WILL THRIVE IN AN ENVIRONMENT THAT:

Provides them with an understanding of true service

Provides them with appropriate boundaries

Provides them with ways to fine-tune their ability to see all sides of a situation

QUESTIONS TO ASK YOUR DIPLOMAT:

What am I choosing to compromise on in this situation? Is it a compromise or a sacrifice?

Is this relationship nurturing and supportive for all parties?

DISILLUSIONIST

Tone

You are able to break down illusions for yourself and others. You can do this through words or by creating images. You can deconstruct yourself and others to the core, which allows for opportunities to rebuild illusions in a different way.

INFLUENTIAL WORDS:

Real

Truth

Illusion

ABILITIES AND TALENTS:

You have a keen sense of what is true and what is fake

You have a talent for seeing the illusions in our world

CONSCIOUSLY EXPERIENCING THIS LANGUAGE:

Revealing illusion in your own reality, then offering that awareness to others

Deconstructing illusions with compassion and love

Understanding the difference between reality and illusion

UNCONSCIOUSLY EXPERIENCING THIS LANGUAGE:

Poking holes in other people's realities without compassion

Being in denial about the illusion that is your reality

Not asking for permission to bring to light a person's illusions

Judging your own world

SIGNS YOU ARE ON THE PATH:

You express the consciousness of love and compassion for yourself and your own life

You wait for permission before sharing and deconstructing an illusion

LANGUAGE ORIENTATION:

The *Disillusionist* is Action/Still. Your Soul has a desire to reflect prior to taking action. It is important that you utilize the stillness to determine what needs to be shifted in your own life, and to determine to "...whether it is appropriate to offer your insights to another individual.

ACCESSING AND ATTRACTING SUPPORT:

Negotiator (Axiom of Quest) – These individuals can teach the *Disillusionist* how to create successful new deals for themselves and others.

Pleasure Seeker (Axiom of Translation) – These individuals can teach the *Disillusionist* how to have fun and not be serious all the time.

Deliberator (Tone) – These individuals are the great decision-makers. They can help the *Disillusionist* fine-tune their reality by identifying where they should deconstruct and where they should let go.

IF YOUR BUSINESS'S TONE IS DISILLUSIONIST:

You are clear about what you offer to your clients

You have clear boundaries

Your company's actions match its words

A CHILD WHO SPEAKS THIS LANGUAGE WILL THRIVE IN AN ENVIRONMENT THAT:

Provides them with the tools to create powerful, sustainable beliefs

Provides them with a sense of safety

Provides them with the tools to create their own reality with love

QUESTIONS TO ASK YOUR DISILLUSIONIST:

What reality do I want to create?

Where am I judging myself or others for an illusion?

DRIVER

Tone

You represent force and motion. You are the one that can guide the movement of any situation. You are an individual that can be trusted to vigorously steer through any situation.

INFLUENTIAL WORDS:

Power

Strength

Movement

ABILITIES AND TALENTS:

You are able to know what action can be taken to create movement in a situation

You have the strength to help complete situations

CONSCIOUSLY EXPERIENCING THIS LANGUAGE:

Understanding that you are "in the driver's seat" because you have an innate ability to guide the movement of a situation with grace

Understanding that you are guiding but not always participating in the movement

Understanding that you are not the movement itself

Being balanced between action and reflection

Understanding what Divine movement can be taken

Understanding when to be patient in a situation and when to step on the gas

Understanding where movement can be created in your own life

Unconsciously experiencing this Language:

Feeling the need to control every situation

Charging through situations without determining if it is for the greatest good of all to do so

Driving without a map

Driving just so you feel like you are "doing something"

Judging the pace of your life

Signs you are on the path:

You maintain balance between action and reflection

You have a sense of where you are driving to

You have let go of control and trust that you are being Divinely guided

Language Orientation:

The *Driver* is Action. Your Soul has a desire to move directly into action. For the *Driver*, it is important that action is taken through Divine inspiration and not just for the sake of action.

Accessing and Attracting Support:

Negotiator (Axiom of Quest) – These individuals can teach the *Driver* how to create successful new deals for themselves and others.

Nurturer (Axiom of Translation) – These individuals can teach the *Driver* how to receive and nurture their gifts and talents.

Carter (Tone) – These individuals carry a message and can provide the right "vehicle" for others to hear that message. They can help the *Driver* understand their unlimited ability to listen to the messages around them.

IF YOUR BUSINESS'S TONE IS DRIVER:

You are clear about what movement the company offers

You have a trusted support staff, including partners and team members that you can trust to help you do the driving

You have created time within the company for reflection, and to set goals or intentions

A CHILD WHO SPEAKS THIS LANGUAGE WILL THRIVE IN AN ENVIRONMENT THAT:

Provides them with balance

Provides them with the skill of patience

Provides them with a deep understanding of what action can be taken

QUESTIONS TO ASK YOUR DRIVER:

Where can I let go of control in order to support my life and/or company?

Where am I trying to force the movement of this situation?

Enchantress/Enchanter

Tone

You are able to use form, energy, and language to delight, influence, charm, inspire, and bewitch. You prefer to give yourself and others opportunities to experience the magic of the Universe.

You understand what can turn yourself and others into heroes/heroines, or into swine.

Influential words:

Magic

Charm

Captivate

Abilities and Talents:

You are able to offer opportunities to tap into the magic of the Universe in order to bring out the best or worst in others

You are able to "see" the hero/heroine in yourself and others

Consciously experiencing this Language:

Utilizing magic with the intention of the greatest good of all

Being able to see and express your own hero or heroine

Utilizing your power for your own life purpose, and your life purpose alone

Providing the opportunity for others to utilize their power for their own life purpose

Allowing the "charms" of the Universe to work through you with balance and harmony

Unconsciously experiencing this Language:

Utilizing your charm and magic for "personal gain" (at the expense of others)

Holding back your power because you are afraid it can hurt or damage others

Being unable to see and feel your heroic qualities

Being unable to feel or see the magic in the Universe

Manipulating others through your "charm"

Signs you are on the path:

You know and utilize your power with the intention for the greatest good of all

You are expressing your own hero or heroine

Language Orientation:

The *Enchantress/Enchanter* is Still. Allowing yourself to be still and reflect will allow you to understand and "be" in the energy of magic and to accept your power more fully.

Accessing and Attracting Support:

Prophet (Axiom of Quest) – These individuals not only deliver messages, they understand what gets to be created in order to deliver each message. They can help the *Enchantress/Enchanter* understand the message of the hero's magic.

Partner (Axiom of Translation) – These individuals are all about creating balanced partnerships. They can help the *Enchantress/Enchanter* not "give away" their power in relationships.

Connoisseur (Tone) – These individuals prefer to go through life full of acceptance. They can help the *Enchantress/Enchanter* accept themselves so they don't manipulate magic for personal gain.

IF YOUR BUSINESS'S TONE IS ENCHANTRESS/ENCHANTER:

You are clear about how the company is using magic

You are clear about what opportunity you are offering others to activate the hero/heroine inside of them

The company's intention is clear and well-stated

A CHILD WHO SPEAKS THIS LANGUAGE WILL THRIVE IN AN ENVIRONMENT THAT:

Provides them with healthy self-esteem

Supports them in being open to possibility and magic

Provides them with models of healthy relationships

QUESTIONS TO ASK YOUR ENCHANTRESS/ENCHANTER:

What is my intention?

Where can I feel and see the magic of the Universe in this situation?

ESCALATOR

Tone

You prefer to experience expansion at a steady and sustainable pace. You escalate, magnify, and amplify energy for the purpose of expansion.

INFLUENTIAL WORDS:

Growth

Sustainable

Energy

ABILITIES AND TALENTS:

You are able to expand and magnify energy to create an expansion

You are able to help yourself and others rise in levels of consciousness at a steady pace with grace

CONSCIOUSLY EXPERIENCING THIS LANGUAGE:

Not being attached to the process of expansion

Maintaining escalation, magnification, and amplification at a steady and graceful pace

Paying attention to your own expansion

Listening to yourself and your Soul for information about your own development

UNCONSCIOUSLY EXPERIENCING THIS LANGUAGE:

Getting too personally involved in another's expansion

Speeding up or slowing down the process of your own or another's expansion

Ignoring the signs of escalation which help you monitor the process, resulting in an experience of expansion as implosion or explosion

Feeling judgmental about your own life

Resisting change and expansion

SIGNS YOU ARE ON THE PATH:

You are aware of your own expansion process

You are creating a steady expansion without judgment

LANGUAGE ORIENTATION:

The *Escalator* is Action/Still. Your Soul has a desire to reflect prior to moving into action. This is important because it will allow you to listen to your Soul to determine what the next Divinely inspired action is, which will allow for a smoother expansion process.

ACCESSING AND ATTRACTING SUPPORT:

Negotiator (Axiom of Quest) – These individuals can teach the *Escalator* how to create successful new deals for themselves and others.

Motivator (Axiom of Translation) – These individuals can help the *Escalator* understand their motivation behind choosing to expand or choosing to be "stuck."

Connoisseur (Tone) – These individuals can help the *Escalator* love and accept themselves more, which will lead to more balanced expansion.

IF YOUR BUSINESS'S TONE IS ESCALATOR:

You are clear about the company's goals

You have a clear plan for structure and growth

You have clear systems in place for continuous expansion

A CHILD WHO SPEAKS THIS LANGUAGE WILL THRIVE IN AN ENVIRONMENT THAT:

Provides them with a strong sense of balance

Provides them with structures for development and growth

Provides them with a strong sense that appropriate change is safe

QUESTIONS TO ASK YOUR ESCALATOR:

Where am I judging my own development and growth?

Where am I trying to stop my own development and growth?

EVOLVER

Tone

You are all about movement, transition, and evolution. You understand that everything has a meaning and that steps are necessary for development. You understand that change is a necessary driving force in life.

INFLUENTIAL WORDS:

Progress

Develop

Synchronicity

ABILITIES AND TALENTS:

You are able to see the steps for expansion

You are skilled at going with the flow of life

CONSCIOUSLY EXPERIENCING THIS LANGUAGE:

Participating with ease in the movements and transitions of your life

Providing support for others in life transitions and developments in a co-creative, healthy way

Understanding your own evolutionary path and following it

Going with the ebb and flow of life

UNCONSCIOUSLY EXPERIENCING THIS LANGUAGE:

Resisting change and evolution

Trying to skip necessary steps in the evolutionary process

Judging your evolutionary process

Trying to take someone else's evolutionary steps

Going against the current

SIGNS YOU ARE ON THE PATH:

You know your own evolutionary path

You move through transitions with ease and grace

LANGUAGE ORIENTATION:

The *Evolver* is Action/Still. Your Soul has a desire to reflect prior to moving into action. It is important for you to access the stillness to really understand the evolutionary steps, and to be aware if you are resisting or trying to skip a step.

ACCESSING AND ATTRACTING SUPPORT:

Peacemaker (Axiom of Quest) – These individuals can help the *Evolver* maintain a sense of peace during each evolutionary step

Herald (Axiom of Translation) – These individuals help bring the news of change. They can help the *Evolver* see change coming.

Bricklayer (Tone) – These individuals can see patterns and help create new ones. They can be a resource for the *Evolver* on how to let go of old patterns and create new ones that will make the evolutionary path smoother.

IF YOUR BUSINESS'S TONE IS EVOLVER:

You understand what evolutionary change you are offering

You have clear steps and processes for others to understand their own evolutionary path and follow it

You understand where evolution and change can happen within the company

A CHILD WHO SPEAKS THIS LANGUAGE WILL THRIVE IN AN ENVIRONMENT THAT:

Helps them develop patience for evolution

Helps them see the necessary steps in situations

Provides them with a strong understanding of their own value

QUESTIONS TO ASK YOUR EVOLVER:

What is the next internal step for my evolution?

What is the next external step for my evolution?

Where am I trying to skip or avoid an evolutionary step?

FIREMAKER

Tone

You provide details that may seem small at first but have a profound effect on evolution. In a sense, you create the spark that ignites a fire.

You are able to be passionate about a subject and spread that passion to others.

INFLUENTIAL WORDS:

Passion

Movement

Eternal

ABILITIES AND TALENTS:

You are able to evoke and ignite passion in others

You are able to maintain a consistent passion for a long time

CONSCIOUSLY EXPERIENCING THIS LANGUAGE:

Understanding what spark to create for an evolution

Knowing what you are passionate about

Spreading your passions to the appropriate individuals

Understanding the essence of life and what individuals need to keep their fire burning

Knowing how to create structure, things, and relationships that will eternally be filled with passion

UNCONSCIOUSLY EXPERIENCING THIS LANGUAGE:

Starting fires for the sake of watching them burn (e.g. creating drama)

Not knowing what will keep your own fire going

Being passionate about things that are not supporting or nurturing your life

Experiencing burnout

SIGNS YOU ARE ON THE PATH:

You know your passions

You know when you are starting to spark a fire

You are keeping your passions fueled without burning yourself out

LANGUAGE ORIENTATION:

The *Firemaker* is Action/Still. It is important to understand where stillness is required prior to taking action.

ACCESSING AND ATTRACTING SUPPORT:

Elemental (Axiom of Quest) – These individuals have an understanding of form and how to utilize it. They can help the *Firemaker* further understand the importance of fire and why people create unnecessary passions.

Apprentice (Axiom of Translation) – These individuals know how to translate what they learn into tangible skills. They can help the *Firemaker* understand what skills are needed in order to keep their fires going.

Escalator (Tone) – These individuals escalate, magnify, and amplify energies for the purpose of expansion. They can help the *Firemaker* understand where to focus in order to expand their passion and keep their fires going.

IF YOUR BUSINESS'S TONE IS FIREMAKER:

You understand the passion of the business and the passions of your employees or staff

You understand where the business is being consumed, unnecessarily starting or putting out fires

You know what individuals require to keep everything alight in the business marketing

You have created appropriate downtime so there isn't burnout in the business

A CHILD WHO SPEAKS THIS LANGUAGE WILL THRIVE IN AN ENVIRONMENT THAT:

Provides them with an assortment of ways to be passionate

Provides them with a structure to maintain their fire

Provides them with tools for trust and faith, so they can live without judgment of their own passions

QUESTIONS TO ASK YOUR FIREMAKER:

What am I truly passionate about?

What fire am I sparking in this situation?

What spark do I get to offer this situation?

GRACEFUL WARRIOR

Tone

You are all about action. You are able to wield the sword with compassion and strength. You know honor, you understand honor, and you recognize the right time to go to battle. You realize how and when to use your power and strength in grace (grace is defined here as the influence or spirit of God operating in humans to regenerate or strengthen them).

INFLUENTIAL WORDS:

Courage

Grace

Honor

ABILITIES AND TALENTS:

You have an unlimited amount of courage and strength

You have a keen sense of right and wrong

CONSCIOUSLY EXPERIENCING THIS LANGUAGE:

Knowing that in every conflict there is a commonality

Knowing that compassion is the greatest tool and feeling it for yourself and others

Knowing when raw strength is the only cause of action

Having a deep connection with the Divine

Allowing for the stillness before taking action

Directing anger appropriately

Understanding that there is strength in vulnerability

Having a keen sense of right and wrong

UNCONSCIOUSLY EXPERIENCING THIS LANGUAGE:

Being ready for a fight

Turning every situation into a war or battle

Berating yourself for not having enough honor or courage

Feeling unsupported because you will not ask for help

Inappropriately directing your anger by exploding or imploding

Refusing to let go of situations or individuals out of a fierce sense of misdirected loyalty

Refusing to see that there is a gray area in some situations

Creating situations to show that you are courageous

Creating conflict or enemies at every turn

Having trouble with authority

SIGNS YOU ARE ON THE PATH:

You have a deep compassion for yourself and others

You know not everything is a fight or a challenge

LANGUAGE ORIENTATION:

The *Graceful Warrior* is Action. Your Soul has a desire to move directly into action. It is key to allow this action to be Divinely inspired.

ACCESSING AND ATTRACTING SUPPORT:

Ambassador (Axiom of Quest) – The *Ambassador's* mission is to be a bridge of love and understanding in order to facilitate benevolent cooperation. They can help the *Graceful Warrior* resolve conflicts without force.

Heart Conscious (Axiom of Translation) – These individuals are heart-centered. They can help the *Graceful Warrior* feel the power of their heart.

Philosopher (Tone) – These individuals prefer to ask questions in order to regulate their lives in ethics, metaphysics, logic, etc. They can help the *Graceful Warrior* meet conflict with a sense of level-headedness.

IF YOUR BUSINESS'S TONE IS GRACEFUL WARRIOR:

You are clear what you are standing for

You have support teams in place that you trust

You have systems in place to receive

A CHILD WHO SPEAKS THIS LANGUAGE WILL THRIVE IN AN ENVIRONMENT THAT:

Provides them with a deep understanding that it is safe to be vulnerable

Provides them with a channel to express their anger appropriately

Provides them with a foundation for connection with the Divine

QUESTIONS TO ASK YOUR GRACEFUL WARRIOR:

Where can I have more compassion for myself and for others?

Where can I allow myself to be vulnerable in this situation in order to build a more intimate relationship with myself and the Divine?

GUARDIAN

Tone

You, by nature, are committed to the protection, security, and preservation of those who are in charge of guarding and protecting others. One of the ways that a *Guardian* helps themselves and others is by creating boundaries that help individuals thrive being their true selves.

You are a watcher and supporter of the way of "being" for yourself and for others.

In general, people will be attracted to your strong and protective nature. The following Soul Languages have a strong affiliation with the *Guardian* because their Soul's desire is to feel support, and they can often feel alone in their leadership activities: *Pilot, Shepherd, Constable, Chieftain, Peacemaker, Prophet,* and *Elemental.*

INFLUENTIAL WORDS:

Guard

Strength

Choice

ABILITIES AND TALENTS:

You are able to offer yourself and others the opportunity to feel safe

You are able to be a powerful support team member

CONSCIOUSLY EXPERIENCING THIS LANGUAGE:

Knowing what boundaries to create for yourself

Understanding that you can only offer protection, support, and security; letting go of attachment to that offer

Feeling safe, protected, and supported in your own life

Having co-creative relationships

UNCONSCIOUSLY EXPERIENCING THIS LANGUAGE:

Not asking permission from others to offer them your help and "protection"

Feeling unsafe in your body and in your life

Judging yourself for your abilities and your talents

Sealing yourself off from the world

Feeling attached to what individuals do with opportunities to be supported and protected

Believing you have to do it all

SIGNS YOU ARE ON THE PATH:

You allow yourself to be supported and loved

You have let go of attachment to the free-will choices of others

LANGUAGE ORIENTATION:

The *Guardian* is Action/Still. Your Soul has a desire to reflect prior to moving into action. It is important that you utilize the stillness to fill your body with the knowing that you are safe before moving into action.

ACCESSING AND ATTRACTING SUPPORT:

Observer (Axiom of Quest) – This individual's mission is to record, observe, and report. They can provide the *Guardian* with observations to help them protect and serve.

Lawmaker (Axiom of Translation) – These individuals help create structures for peace. They can help the *Guardian* create new beliefs that sustain peace in their body.

Capitalist (Tone) – These individuals are able to increase abundance. They can help the *Guardian* create safety for money and abundance.

IF YOUR BUSINESS'S TONE IS GUARDIAN:

You have clear boundaries with your clients

You understand what form of protection or safety you are offering to others

You are allowing others to support you and the company

A CHILD WHO SPEAKS THIS LANGUAGE WILL THRIVE IN AN ENVIRONMENT THAT:

Provides them with a structure for asking before doing

Provides them with a structure for feeling safe and secure

Provides them with examples of healthy, co-creative relationships

QUESTIONS TO ASK YOUR GUARDIAN:

Where do I not feel safe?

Where am I judging myself and my gifts?

Heartfelt Artist

Tone

You create art with intuition, with feeling and emotion. Your art is formed through the energy of your heart and Soul. A *Heartfelt Artist* visibly displays their essence in their work. Your artwork seems to be alive with emotion and feeling.

You have a desire to display in your art how you feel, and want to help others emote through your art.

Influential words:

Heartfelt

Create

Inspired

Abilities and talents:

You are able to create beauty from anything

You are able to capture emotion and display it for others in a powerful way

Consciously experiencing this Language:

Creating powerful works of art without struggle or compromise

Expressing your emotions appropriately

Giving yourself sacred time to create

Being comfortable in the spotlight

Setting appropriate emotional boundaries

Knowing what you desire to create and the medium in which to do it

UNCONSCIOUSLY EXPERIENCING THIS LANGUAGE:

Struggling with the creative process

Feeling stuck or uninspired

Stuffing your emotions, or expressing them inappropriately

Hiding your talents

Not allowing yourself proper time for creation

SIGNS YOU ARE ON THE PATH:

You have sacred time to create

You are expressing your emotions appropriately

You are willing to be seen

LANGUAGE ORIENTATION:

The *Heartfelt Artist* is Action/Still. Your Soul has a desire to reflect prior to creating. It is important that you allow yourself time in the stillness and not "push" the creative process.

ACCESSING AND ATTRACTING SUPPORT:

Genius (Axiom of Quest) – This individual has the supreme intelligence to create new ways of thinking. They can provide the *Heartfelt Artist* with new ways of looking at things.

Hero (Axiom of Translation) – These individual have an innate ability to complete a task that might seem overwhelming to others. They can help the *Heartfelt Artist* by providing support and courage to stop hiding and to fully express themselves.

Closer (Tone) – These individuals innately know when something is complete. They can provide the *Heartfelt Artist* with the understanding of how to "let go."

IF YOUR BUSINESS'S TONE IS HEARTFELT ARTIST:

You need to understand the creative process of the business

You need to understand what spotlight the business wants to be in

You need to understand what emotions are being expressed through the business, and how

A CHILD WHO SPEAKS THIS LANGUAGE WILL THRIVE IN AN ENVIRONMENT THAT:

Provides them with the knowledge that it is safe and prosperous to create

Provides them with appropriate ways to express their emotions

Provides them with opportunities to find and nurture their art

QUESTIONS TO ASK YOUR HEARTFELT ARTIST:

What do I desire to create?

Where am I hiding my talents and why?

Industrialist

Tone

You focus not on what can be done with human hands but rather what can be done by letting go and working with the mechanics of the brain.

You have an innate ability to utilize the power of the mind. You prefer to guide others from a way of living that might be archaic in nature to a more sophisticated way of operating.

INFLUENTIAL WORDS:

Individual and Whole

Connection

Transformation

ABILITIES AND TALENTS:

You are able to understand how one way of doing something can be replaced with a more aware and productive way

You are able to understand where the weakest link in a system is and how it can be updated to benefit the whole

CONSCIOUSLY EXPERIENCING THIS LANGUAGE:

Understanding how the many components of a system can work in unison to achieve superior results

Being able to quickly discern where a system's "weakest link" is located, and knowing how to strengthen it in a manner that supports the whole

Knowing that any system can be updated and adapted

Knowing the difference between producing and creating

UNCONSCIOUSLY EXPERIENCING THIS LANGUAGE:

Focusing too narrowly, which can lead to blind spots when trying to see the whole of things

Updating just for the sake of updating

Judging yourself and others because "systems" aren't being updated quickly enough

Creating revolutions as a form of distraction

SIGNS YOU ARE ON THE PATH:

You know what systems in your own world can be updated

You are loving and patient with yourself and others

LANGUAGE ORIENTATION:

The *Industrialist* is Action/Still. It is important you take the time to listen and reflect before moving into action. This will allow you to understand more of the system.

ACCESSING AND ATTRACTING SUPPORT:

Observer (Axiom of Quest) – These individuals can provide insight on where the *Industrialist* can let go.

Emerald (Axiom of Translation) – These individuals can help the *Industrialist* understand what in their world can be realigned.

Agent (Tone) – These individuals have an understanding of their power and a desire to express it. They know that they have the ability and power to create their own lives. These individuals can help the *Industrialist* accept and understand their own power.

IF YOUR BUSINESS'S TONE IS INDUSTRIALIST:

You understand the systems of the business and what "weak links" get to be updated

You have a clear sense of what the business is producing and creating

You have a clear direction and focus

A CHILD WHO SPEAKS THIS LANGUAGE WILL THRIVE IN AN ENVIRONMENT THAT:

Provides them with tools to utilize their talents of seeing and understanding "weak links" in a loving and compassionate way

Provides them with beliefs and structures to be without judgment for themselves

Provides them with ways to feel supported

Provides them with ways to gain clarity and focus

QUESTIONS TO ASK YOUR INDUSTRIALIST:

What weak link am I feeling judgmental about?

What system in my own life is currently outdated, and how can it be updated to be more productive?

INTELLECT

Tone

You rely on the power of the mind to understand yourself, your surroundings, and others.

The mind is the key to understanding all with the intellect. You are keen on acquiring knowledge and facts in order to process the world, using these facts as a way to understand how the world works.

This Tone is shared by the largest number of Souls on this planet.

INFLUENTIAL WORDS:

Mind

Understand

Leading

ABILITIES AND TALENTS:

You are able to understand and process facts quickly

You are able to acquire a vast amount of knowledge and facts

CONSCIOUSLY EXPERIENCING THIS LANGUAGE:

Including the heart and spirit in processing facts

Being aware and responding appropriately to what you are feeling

Understanding your connection to the Divine

Utilizing this connection for the appropriate gathering of knowledge

Understanding the different parts of the mind

UNCONSCIOUSLY EXPERIENCING THIS LANGUAGE:

Basing your decisions solely on the perceptions of the ego

Closing yourself off emotionally and/or spiritually

Seeing only the facts, not truly understanding them with body, mind, and spirit

SIGNS YOU ARE ON THE PATH:

You have integrated spirit into your process and are working with body, mind, and spirit

You are open-minded

LANGUAGE ORIENTATION:

The *Intellect* is Action/Still. Your Soul has a desire to reflect prior to taking action.

This helps you to determine what you are feeling and "check in" for additional information from the Divine before moving into action.

ACCESSING AND ATTRACTING SUPPORT:

Genius (Axiom of Quest) – The mission of the *Genius* is to usher in a new way of existence. The *Genius* can help the *Intellect* understand how intelligence can be the spark of Soulful evolution and change.

Hero (Axiom of Translation) – These individuals have an innate ability to complete a task that might seem overwhelming or inconceivable to others. They can help the *Intellect* understand that emotions do not have to overwhelm them.

Beekeeper (Tone) – These individuals are the keepers of productivity (mental, spiritual, and physical). They can help the *Intellect* learn how to communicate effectively and work harmoniously with body, mind, and spirit.

IF YOUR BUSINESS'S TONE IS INTELLECT:

You are clear about the knowledge you are presenting

You are open to new ideas

You have created channels and systems to receive

A CHILD WHO SPEAKS THIS LANGUAGE WILL THRIVE IN AN ENVIRONMENT THAT:

Provides them with the safety to express their emotions

Provides them with a process to allow their mind to follow their heart

Provides them with the understanding that there is more to see than just the facts

QUESTIONS TO ASK YOUR INTELLECT:

What do I think about this situation and how do I feel about this situation?

What knowledge do I have that will help me understand and process this situation?

INVESTIGATOR

Tone

You diligently research a subject. You search out and examine life by close inspection in an attempt to understand the mystery of things. You are quite skilled at unveiling what most other people miss in their observation of things.

INFLUENTIAL WORDS:

Search

Examine

Understand

ABILITIES AND TALENTS:

You are able to see and unveil what others miss

You are able to follow a lead to see where it ends up and how it can support you or others

CONSCIOUSLY EXPERIENCING THIS LANGUAGE:

Revealing the multiple layers of life for yourself and others

Understanding that some mystery is essential for the magic of life

Understanding what to investigate and why

Explaining the results of your investigations without fear or attachment

Asking questions that allow others the opportunity to discover

UNCONSCIOUSLY EXPERIENCING THIS LANGUAGE:

Examining life in so much detail that you are not living your own life

Getting bogged down in the examining of things and using this for sabotage

Having attachment to what others do with the information you present to them from your investigations

Getting caught up in conspiracy theories

Interrogating others rather than asking gentle questions

SIGNS YOU ARE ON THE PATH:

You know when to start and when to stop an investigation

You are comfortable presenting your investigations to others without worry or concern about their reactions

You are experiencing the magic of life without needing to investigate it

LANGUAGE ORIENTATION:

The *Investigator* is Action/Still. Your Soul has a desire to reflect prior to taking action. This reflection will help you to determine what needs to be investigated, when an investigation is complete, and when you get to move on from an investigation.

ACCESSING AND ATTRACTING SUPPORT:

Counselor (Axiom of Quest) – These individuals can help provide the *Investigator* with the ability to understand a course of action that their investigations can take.

Apprentice (Axiom of Translation) – These individuals can help the *Investigator* with the nuts and bolts of how things work. This will help them understand how the details of an investigation fit into the big picture.

Guardian (Tone) – These individuals can help the *Investigator* create appropriate boundaries for their investigations to ensure that they are not over-investigating.

IF YOUR BUSINESS'S TONE IS INVESTIGATOR:

You need to know what you are investigating and why

You need to create systems that allow information to be presented without attachment

You are clear with clients what they would like you to investigate

A CHILD WHO SPEAKS THIS LANGUAGE WILL THRIVE IN AN ENVIRONMENT THAT:

Provides them with an understanding of appropriate avenues for investigation

Provides them with the ability to communicate with others what their investigation yields

Provides them with the knowledge that they are of value no matter what happens during an investigation

QUESTIONS TO ASK YOUR INVESTIGATOR:

Why am I choosing this investigation?

What might I be avoiding by diving deeper into another investigation?

LIBRARIAN

Tone

You prefer to file and reference information. You are able to access this material as a resource for others or for yourself.

INFLUENTIAL WORDS:

Knowledge

Information

Catalog

ABILITIES AND TALENTS:

You are able to collect and access vast amounts of information

You are able to provide yourself and others with resources for expansion through knowledge

CONSCIOUSLY EXPERIENCING THIS LANGUAGE:

Collecting information with respect for the human element

Utilizing the information you collect to create a more expansive life for yourself and others

Living life not only through knowledge but also through experience

Recognizing when no more information is needed on a subject

Participating in the physical experience of your life

UNCONSCIOUSLY EXPERIENCING THIS LANGUAGE:

Dedicating yourself to filing information to the point of not fully participating in life's pleasures

Not knowing how to access the information within

Filing and categorizing your knowledge without fully integrating it into your life and Soul

Feeling as if you will never know enough

SIGNS YOU ARE ON THE PATH:

You know what knowledge you require to expand your life

You are fully participating in your life

You know and understand your own value

LANGUAGE ORIENTATION:

The *Librarian* is Still. Your Soul has a desire to reflect. This gives you time to absorb the knowledge you are collecting. It is important that you do not get stuck in the stillness or it may lead to feeling as if you are not participating in life to the fullest.

ACCESSING AND ATTRACTING SUPPORT:

Pioneer (Axiom of Quest) – These individuals help others forge new paths for themselves. They can help the *Librarian* embrace new experiences.

Purveyor (Axiom of Translation) – These individuals have access to an unlimited supply of resources. They can help the *Librarian* locate additional resources to help with the collection of knowledge through experience.

Firemaker (Tone) – These individuals help others spark their passions. They can help the *Librarian* understand what makes them feel passionate.

IF YOUR BUSINESS'S TONE IS LIBRARIAN:

You know what information you are offering your audience

You have a clear system for how your audience can access that information

You know what information the company requires to expand

A CHILD WHO SPEAKS THIS LANGUAGE WILL THRIVE IN AN ENVIRONMENT THAT:

Provides them with an understanding that they are "good enough"

Provides them with a balance between quiet learning and learning by action

Provides them with educational support

QUESTIONS TO ASK YOUR LIBRARIAN:

What knowledge can I access in this situation?

Where can I participate more in my own life?

Mortar Maker

Tone

You provide substance to fill the gaps and bind situations together. You are the one who is able to see that we are not all separate. You understand that we are one and you can provide the guidance, words, images, etc. to help others see that as well.

Love is the substance you offer others. It provides what is necessary to maintain the unity of an individual, situation, or community.

Influential words:

Unity

Love

Community

Abilities and talents:

You are able to quickly feel the deep love of the Universe

You know we are all one and can explain that to others

Consciously experiencing this Language:

Being able to access the love inside you instantly

Guiding others to see the love inside of them without attachment

Having a deep understanding of yourself and the Divine

UNCONSCIOUSLY EXPERIENCING THIS LANGUAGE:

Being unable to tap into the love that binds us all together

Feeling alone and separate

Judging yourself and others

SIGNS YOU ARE ON THE PATH:

You know and feel your own value and love

You have a supportive and loving community

You know you are an individual but also part of the whole

LANGUAGE ORIENTATION:

The *Mortar Maker* is Still. Your Soul has a desire to reflect. Using the stillness to listen is the key to understanding and feeling the substance that binds us all together – Love.

ACCESSING AND ATTRACTING SUPPORT:

Equalizer (Axiom of Quest) – These individuals can help the *Mortar Maker* understand what choices they get to make in order to maintain balance and love for their own life.

Herald (Axiom of Translation) – These individuals bring forth information for change. They can help the *Mortar Maker* bring forth information for love.

Analyst (Tone) – These individuals can help the *Mortar Maker* describe the feeling of love to individuals who are more left-brained in nature.

IF YOUR BUSINESS'S TONE IS MORTAR MAKER:

You are clear about what you are offering your clients

You have good support teams in place

You have policies in place that are nurturing in nature and provide the opportunity for others to feel supported

A CHILD WHO SPEAKS THIS LANGUAGE WILL THRIVE IN AN ENVIRONMENT THAT:

Provides them with a deep knowing that they are loved

Provides them with a foundation for unity

Provides them with the tools to be aware of their choices

QUESTIONS TO ASK YOUR MORTAR MAKER:

What does the consciousness of love feel like inside of me?

Where am I creating a feeling of being separate?

OLYMPIAN

Tone

You prefer to bring together individuals from all walks of life for a common purpose, action, idea, thought, or creation. You prefer to do this without struggle, friction, or argument because you understand that we are all one.

The *Olympian* is an embodiment of what all humans possess here on earth: being human. Through your words and actions, you can illustrate for others that humanity is Divine and that oneness can be a great force for the greater good.

INFLUENTIAL WORDS:

Unity

Individuality

Greatest

ABILITIES AND TALENTS:

You are able to bring together many different individuals for a common purpose

You are able to see and bring out the best in each human being

You are able to create thoughts and ideas for unification

CONSCIOUSLY EXPERIENCING THIS LANGUAGE:

Understanding that even prejudice within you can, through compassion, be transformed for the benefit of mankind

Understanding how you are both an individual and part of a whole

Feeling love for all parts of yourself

Understanding that we each have many faces and parts of ourselves, and that each face or part is a reflection of humanity

Feeling complete and whole by fostering unification of Soul and body

Feeling and understanding the greatness within yourself and others

UNCONSCIOUSLY EXPERIENCING THIS LANGUAGE:

Feeling separate from others

Fostering division rather than unification within yourself and others

Judging your own humanity

Losing faith in humans and our capabilities

SIGNS YOU ARE ON THE PATH:

You know what brings out the best in yourself

You have a sense of the common objective of the group that you are bringing together

LANGUAGE ORIENTATION:

The *Olympian* is Action/Still. Your Soul has a desire to reflect prior to moving into action. This reflection process allows for the *Olympian* to feel the greatness within themselves and others.

ACCESSING AND ATTRACTING SUPPORT:

Negotiator (Axiom of Quest) – These individuals can teach the *Olympian* how to create successful new deals for themselves and others.

Lawmaker (Axiom of Translation) – These individuals can teach the *Olympian* to create structures of peace for themselves and others.

Connoisseur (Tone) – These individuals are all about acceptance. They can help the *Olympian* accept their humanity more.

IF YOUR BUSINESS'S TONE IS OLYMPIAN:

You are clear about what is expected of each employee, client, etc.

You clearly communicate the mission or focus of the company

You have appropriate systems in place to highlight, praise, and reward both employees and company accomplishments

A CHILD WHO SPEAKS THIS LANGUAGE WILL THRIVE IN AN ENVIRONMENT THAT:

Supports their friendships with individuals from different walks of life

Provides them with tools to support their leadership qualities

Provides them with a structure to feel as if they "belong"

QUESTIONS TO ASK YOUR OLYMPIAN:

Where am I judging my own humanity in this situation?

What is the common objective or focus in this situation?

OUTSIDER

Tone

You are able to disconnect and place yourself outside situations in a way that enables you to determine, for yourself and for others, appropriate boundaries and opportunities for change.

You command a clear understanding of conformity and non-conformity as concepts. You understand that conformity must have boundaries because it means being "like the group," and just beyond that line lies non-conformity and individual self-expression.

INFLUENTIAL WORDS:

Group

Individual

Boundary

ABILITIES AND TALENTS:

You have a talent for being able to be outside a situation in order to see the whole of it

You have a keen awareness of what it means to be both an individual and part of the group

CONSCIOUSLY EXPERIENCING THIS LANGUAGE:

Understanding that being outside is not the same as being alone

Attracting events and situations where you feel included

Knowing you can be outside a situation and still feel whole and part of the community

Understanding that your individual self-expression is not a reason to feel alone

Understanding how to be an individual within a group

Knowing that each member of a group adds to its whole

UNCONSCIOUSLY EXPERIENCING THIS LANGUAGE:

Secluding yourself from others and feeling lonely

Feeling unsupported by the whole

Failing to maintain boundaries

Enforcing boundaries so much that you do not receive

SIGNS YOU ARE ON THE PATH:

You have appropriate boundaries

You have attracted, found, and accepted your community

You feel supported

LANGUAGE ORIENTATION:

The *Outsider* is Action/Still. Your Soul has a desire to be still and reflect prior to moving into action. It is important that this stillness be balanced or this can create unnecessary friction, getting stuck outside of situations.

ACCESSING AND ATTRACTING SUPPORT:

Elemental (Axiom of Quest) – These individuals understand the nature of things, how things are created and formed. They can help the *Outsider* see what each member of the group has in common.

Messenger (Axiom of Translation) – These individuals are able to decode the messages of the Universe. They can help the *Outsider* understand what messages can help them move from outside the circle to inside of it.

Artisan (Tone) – These individuals have the talent to take on new skills and abilities easily. They can help the *Outsider* understand what skills and talents they have, and which ones they get to develop.

IF YOUR BUSINESS'S TONE IS OUTSIDER:

You know where the appropriate boundaries are

You understand who your community is

You understand what makes the community a unique part of the whole

A CHILD WHO SPEAKS THIS LANGUAGE WILL THRIVE IN AN ENVIRONMENT THAT:

Lets them know that they are valued, supported, and accepted

Provides them with an understanding of when they are unnecessarily putting themselves outside of a situation

Provides them with strong, appropriate boundaries

QUESTIONS TO ASK YOUR OUTSIDER:

How can I express my individuality in this situation while still feeling part of the whole?

What do I get to let go of in order to attract more support?

PASSAGE INVENTOR

Tone

You prefer to create routes and corridors in situations where there is no obvious direction or path.

You prefer to create from imagination, your own way of hearing the Universe, and to utilize this source in formulating and creating.

INFLUENTIAL WORDS:

Passageway

Course

Perceive

ABILITIES AND TALENTS:

You are able to see the multiple layers of situations in order for a new course to be created

You are able to create a new course with the power of the mind

CONSCIOUSLY EXPERIENCING THIS LANGUAGE:

Moving fearlessly into invention

Knowing what new routes to take on your own journey

Accepting the choices other individuals make for their own journeys

Knowing that all routes and corridors lead to you knowing yourself and the Divine

Understanding clearly how to create a new corridor or passage

UNCONSCIOUSLY EXPERIENCING THIS LANGUAGE:

Being afraid of rejection or criticism for inventing new ways

Fearing that you will be left behind

Fearing that you will be on the journey alone

Being attached to the way in which others participate in their journey

SIGNS YOU ARE ON THE PATH:

You are always discovering more about yourself

You are without attachment

You move easily through fear

LANGUAGE ORIENTATION:

The *Passage Inventor* is Action/Still. Your Soul has a desire to achieve harmony between reflection and action. It is important that you allow for the stillness before moving into action.

ACCESSING AND ATTRACTING SUPPORT:

Negotiator (Axiom of Quest) – These individuals help others create "new deals." They can help the *Passage Inventor* understand how to create win-win scenarios.

Monk (Axiom of Translation) – These individuals understand about living according to a rule or principle. They can help the *Passage Inventor* stay the course.

Dionysian (Tone) – These individuals are all about living life through experiences. They can help the *Passage Inventor* fully participate in life.

IF YOUR BUSINESS'S TONE IS PASSAGE INVENTOR:

You clearly communicate the company's talent for innovation

You have structures in place to allow for the flexibility of trying something new

You have supportive partners who are on board with the company's innovation

A CHILD WHO SPEAKS THIS LANGUAGE WILL THRIVE IN AN ENVIRONMENT THAT:

Provides them with the opportunity to try new ways of tackling situations

Provides them with consistent nurturing support

Provides them with good communication skills to support their unique view of the world

QUESTIONS TO ASK YOUR PASSAGE INVENTOR:

What new course of action can be taken in this situation?

What am I afraid of that is preventing me from inventing something new?

PHILOSOPHER

Tone

You prefer to live your life asking questions and creating theories for profound questions about the Universe. These questions may be in a number of areas, including ethics, metaphysics, logic, etc.

Often these questions can be the "central ideas" for a transformation or movement in your life and the lives of others.

INFLUENTIAL WORDS:

Values

Beliefs

Questions

ABILITIES AND TALENTS:

You are able to be rational and calm even in difficult circumstances

You are able to ask questions that produce a discovery for inner knowledge

CONSCIOUSLY EXPERIENCING THIS LANGUAGE:

Approaching life and situations with composure and level-headedness

Asking "big questions" and then living your life by the answers

Knowing when no more questions need to be asked

Utilizing your own wisdom to consciously create your life

Taking appropriate action and following through

Consulting the Universe and then following through with appropriate action

Understanding the importance of creating deep intimate connections

UNCONSCIOUSLY EXPERIENCING THIS LANGUAGE:

Using your questions and your mind to cut yourself off from others and from life

Having trouble making commitments or taking action

"Sitting on the fence" or not moving into appropriate action

Being full of judgment and self-righteousness for yourself or others

Hiding out in your belief system

Using your "philosophy" to keep you separate and alone

SIGNS YOU ARE ON THE PATH:

You know what questions to ask yourself for your own inner knowledge

You know how to stay calm in difficult situations

You are using your wisdom to live a conscious life

LANGUAGE ORIENTATION:

The *Philosopher* is Still. Your Soul has a desire to reflect. This reflection is important because it allows you to have a conversation with the Universe.

ACCESSING AND ATTRACTING SUPPORT:

Peacemaker (Axiom of Quest) – The *Peacemaker's* mission is to maintain a sense of peace within. They can help the *Philosopher* find additional calmness within.

Motivator (Axiom of Translation) – These individuals understand what motivates themselves and others. They can help the *Philosopher* understand their personal motivation for asking the big questions (out of fear or for expansion).

Conductor (Tone) – These individuals prefer to bring out the best within each member of the community. They can help the *Philosopher* understand how to "work" within a community.

IF YOUR BUSINESS'S TONE IS PHILOSOPHER:

You understand when to stop asking questions and move into action

You understand what "big" questions you are asking of your clients/customers

You understand the benefit of creating appropriate support teams and partners

A CHILD WHO SPEAKS THIS LANGUAGE WILL THRIVE IN AN ENVIRONMENT THAT:

Provides them with opportunities to ask questions

Provides them with a forum to discuss and listen to others express their own beliefs

Provides them with a process for knowing when to take action

QUESTIONS TO ASK YOUR PHILOSOPHER:

What question can I ask in this situation that will help me understand it more fully?

Where am I afraid of making a commitment, and why?

PILOT

Tone

You prefer to be the guide for a course of action that is otherwise uncharted or difficult. You provide the opportunity for others to move quickly through uncharted territories.

You prefer to soar as high as you can, without fear and without doubt.

INFLUENTIAL WORDS:

Uncharted

Route

Soar

ABILITIES AND TALENTS:

You are able to create a feeling of safety for yourself and others

You are able to guide others in their actions

CONSCIOUSLY EXPERIENCING THIS LANGUAGE:

Escorting yourself and others through uncharted territories with a feeling of safety, certainty, and confidence

Allowing yourself and others to access their full potential to reach their apex

Feeling safe in your body

Understanding and embracing your own gifts and talents

Moving forward with Divine inspiration, knowing that you are provided for and protected by the Universe

Unconsciously experiencing this Language:

Feeling unsafe in your own body

Feeling unsupported by the Universe

Creating situations in your life that keep you from feeling safe

Being reckless

Feeling like you are off course

Signs you are on the path:

You know what uncharted course to take and know that you will be safe

You know what actions to take for yourself

You feel safe and supported

Language Orientation:

The *Pilot* is Action/Still. Your Soul has a desire to reflect prior to moving into action. This will allow you to create a more profound feeling of safety in your body before moving into an uncharted action.

Accessing and Attracting Support:

Prophet (Axiom of Quest) – These individuals not only understand a message, they also know how to deliver it. They can help the *Pilot* understand their own messages better.

Monk (Axiom of Translation) – These individuals are about living according to a particular principle and understanding the stillness. They can help the *Pilot* be more comfortable with stillness.

Collaborator (Tone) – These individuals are all about true collaboration. They can help the *Pilot* work better in a group.

Also see the *Guardian* (Tone), page 363.

IF YOUR BUSINESS'S TONE IS PILOT:

You are clear in your communication about what opportunities you offer to your clients to create safety for themselves

You are clear about what uncharted territories you are navigating and have a system in place to explore them at a steady and appropriate pace

You have a clear process in place for taking action

A CHILD WHO SPEAKS THIS LANGUAGE WILL THRIVE IN AN ENVIRONMENT THAT:

Provides them with opportunities to feel safe in their body

Provides them with opportunities to take risks

Honors their belief that they can reach unlimited heights

QUESTIONS TO ASK YOUR PILOT:

What course of action can I take here that is unique?

Where do I not feel safe in this situation?

PRODUCER/PROVIDER

Tone

You prefer to produce and provide. These individuals are masters at using creative energy in different ways to produce and provide for themselves and others. You innately understand how energy is generated from thought and becomes form via the creative process.

In receiving the creative energy of the Universe, you understand how to transform that energy into solid form (*Producer*), and how to take that creation and use it to provide for your needs and the needs of others (*Provider*).

INFLUENTIAL WORDS:

Focus

Allow

Create

ABILITIES AND TALENTS:

You are able to produce or provide something out of "nothing"

You are able to understand how to turn thought and energy into form and action

CONSCIOUSLY EXPERIENCING THIS LANGUAGE:

Being balanced in your male and female energies

Understanding what you wish to bring into manifestation

Allowing the Universe to be your great provider

Taking action with Divine inspiration

Co-creating with the Universe

Unconsciously experiencing this Language:

Feeling as if you have to do it all

Trying to "force" creation

Being unclear about what you wish to produce or provide for yourself

Feeling angry and resentful

Being out of balance with your masculine and feminine energies

Signs you are on the path:

You know what you wish to create for yourself and what you will need to bring that into form

You are balanced in your male and female energies

You are aware of what you are bringing into form

Language Orientation:

The *Producer/Provider* is Action/Still. Your Soul has a preference for reflection prior to moving into action. This will allow you to access the Divine to help with manifestation.

Accessing and Attracting Support:

Prophet (Axiom of Quest) – These individuals not only understand a message, they know how to deliver it. They can help the *Producer/Provider* understand what "message" they wish to express with their creations.

Motivator (Axiom of Translation) – These individuals help motivate others to take a leap of faith. They can help the *Producer/Provider* understand what is motivating them to create.

Conductor (Tone) – These individuals are born leaders and help bring out the best in each member of a community. They can help bring out the best in the *Producer/Provider* in order to help them with the manifestation process.

IF YOUR BUSINESS'S TONE IS PRODUCER/PROVIDER:

You are clear about what the company is creating or offering others the opportunity to create

You are clear about what the company is supplying a place to pursue

You have clear support systems in place

A CHILD WHO SPEAKS THIS LANGUAGE WILL THRIVE IN AN ENVIRONMENT THAT:

Provides them with opportunities to give and receive

Provides them with opportunities to take inspired action

Allows them to feel safe expressing their desires and needs

QUESTIONS TO ASK YOUR PRODUCER/PROVIDER:

What does my Soul desire to create?

Where am I trying to "force" the creative process?

Where do I feel unsupported by the Universe in my creation?

PURIST

Tone

You prefer to remain true to your Spirit. You pass up or pass by anything that may dilute, adulterate, or influence you. You embrace and live in tradition.

INFLUENTIAL WORDS:

Pure

Authentic

Essence

ABILITIES AND TALENTS:

You are able to see the pure essence in everything

You are able to align yourself to be guided purely by Spirit

CONSCIOUSLY EXPERIENCING THIS LANGUAGE:

Continually discovering more about your Spirit

Understanding that your truth is not everyone's truth

Incorporating both old and new traditions into your life

Understanding that your Spirit is always expanding, and that what is true for you today might not be true for you tomorrow

Forgiving yourself if you step out of your truth

Retuning your essence to release those situations, beliefs, or feelings that are not part of your Spirit

Unconsciously experiencing this Language:

Judging yourself and others

Being fixated or controlling

Feeling self-righteous

Not forgiving yourself for your own humanity

Letting traditions hold you back

Signs you are on the path:

You are without judgment

You are open to discovering more about your Soul

You are flexible and allow for other truths without having to take them on

Language Orientation:

The *Purist* is Still. Your Soul has a desire for reflection. This allows you to understand what your truth is in each situation you encounter.

Accessing and Attracting Support:

Pioneer (Axiom of Quest) – These individuals help others forge new roads for themselves. They can help the *Purist* create new traditions in their life.

Monk (Axiom of Translation) – These individuals are about living according to a particular principle and understanding the stillness. They can help the *Purist* understand that their truth and traditions are not everyone's truth and traditions.

Connoisseur (Tone) – These individuals are all about acceptance. They can help the *Purist* accept themselves more, which will also help them to accept others more.

IF YOUR BUSINESS'S TONE IS PURIST:

You clearly express the company's truth

You have structures in place that are balanced between new and old ways

You provide the space for your employees to understand and relay their own truths

A CHILD WHO SPEAKS THIS LANGUAGE WILL THRIVE IN AN ENVIRONMENT THAT:

Provides them with supportive traditions

Provides them with a sense of awe for discovery

Provides them with a healthy foundation for forgiveness

QUESTIONS TO ASK YOUR PURIST:

What is my truth in this situation?

What can I let go of in this situation in order to express my truth more fully?

RAVEN

Tone

You are magical by nature. You are able to share through your words and your actions the miracles of rebirth and creation. You bring great knowledge and experience of the life cycle.

Your main focus is to translate for others the joy you see in the life cycle.

INFLUENTIAL WORDS:

Magical

Rebirth

Joy

ABILITIES AND TALENTS:

You are able to see the joy in every cycle and situation of life

You understand how to create magic and provide opportunities for others to do so as well

CONSCIOUSLY EXPERIENCING THIS LANGUAGE:

Being illuminated by the light and joy of rebirth and creation

Understanding that you are the "magic maker" and teaching others how to create their own magic

Moving through the cycles of life with ease and grace

Seeing the magic in heaven and earth

UNCONSCIOUSLY EXPERIENCING THIS LANGUAGE:

Being afraid of the different cycles of life

Feeling unable to express joy in the processes of life

Feeling stuck in a vicious circle of judgment

Being unable to feel or see the joy and magic in heaven and on earth

Creating based solely on another person's desires, wants, or needs

SIGNS YOU ARE ON THE PATH:

You know what fills your Soul with joy

You know that magic requires stillness

You are illuminating any darkness in your life with the magic of the light

LANGUAGE ORIENTATION:

The *Raven* is Still. Your Soul has a desire to create from a place of stillness or reflection. It is important that proper time is given for stillness so you can understand what Divine inspiration to take action on.

ACCESSING AND ATTRACTING SUPPORT:

Elemental (Axiom of Quest) – These individuals have an understanding of form and how to work with it. They can help the *Raven* understand how to co-create and access magic.

Hero (Axiom of Translation) – These individuals understand the innate power of love. They can illustrate the intense magic that comes from using love as a fuel.

Passage Inventor (Tone) – These individuals can create routes and paths where there seem to be no obvious ones. They can help the *Raven* see new pathways of magic.

IF YOUR BUSINESS'S TONE IS RAVEN:

You need to know what experience of magic you are providing your customers or clients with

You need to understand how you are helping your clients understand the cycle of life

You have to know what structure you are providing to show others the joy of the life cycle

You have to understand when to be still (to receive or reflect) and when to create movement or action

A CHILD WHO SPEAKS THIS LANGUAGE WILL THRIVE IN AN ENVIRONMENT THAT:

Provides them with an understanding of the joy of the life cycle

Provides them with beliefs and structures to support their talents and their desire to feel and see the magic of life

Provides them with tools for trust and faith so they can live without judgment for themselves and others

QUESTIONS TO ASK YOUR RAVEN:

Where am I not feeling or seeing the joy of this situation?

How can I access magic in this situation or relationship?

REALIST

Tone

You prefer to view and represent the world as it really is and be grounded in the fullness and richness of it.

You reflect life as you experience it and co-create with that reality.

INFLUENTIAL WORDS:

Actual

Tangible

True

ABILITIES AND TALENTS:

You are able to utilize all five senses at once in order to experience reality as vibrant

You are able to express this vibrancy to others in a way that they can see, feel, and hear

CONSCIOUSLY EXPERIENCING THIS LANGUAGE:

Being grounded and fully participating in life

Experiencing the miracle of life as a part of reality

Understanding that reality is your own construction

Fully accepting that you are creating your own reality

Offering your views to others, without attachment, in order to help them move from illusion or self-denial to creating a more powerful reality

Unconsciously experiencing this Language:

Basing your life on facts alone, not allowing for the creation of the Universe

Not being fully grounded in your body, avoiding reality

Judging your life or another's

Considering your reality the basis of all truth

Signs you are on the path:

You are clear about the illusions in your own life

You are open to the miracles of life

You have accepted that you are creating your own reality

Language Orientation:

The *Realist* is Still. Your Soul prefers to reflect. This reflection allows you to participate in the stillness of reality.

Accessing and Attracting Support:

Pioneer (Axiom of Quest) – These individuals create new roads for themselves and others. They can help the *Realist* see new roads for their own reality.

Image Maker (Axiom of Translation) – These individuals see the essence of a being and then help bring that essence into reality. They can help the *Realist* bring more of their own Soul into reality.

Collaborator (Tone) – These individuals are all about true collaboration. They can help the *Realist* co-create with the Universe.

IF YOUR BUSINESS'S TONE IS REALIST:

You are clear what reality the company is offering

You allow space for creation and miracles within the structure of the company

You hold the company appropriately responsible for the creation of its own reality

A CHILD WHO SPEAKS THIS LANGUAGE WILL THRIVE IN AN ENVIRONMENT THAT:

Provides them with opportunities to explore their five senses

Provides them with a sense of wonder to help build a belief in miracles

Provides them with a practice of being grounded in their own body

QUESTIONS TO ASK YOUR REALIST:

Why am I not accepting the reality of this situation?

Where am I not seeing the miracle of this situation?

Ringmaster

Tone

You prefer to be in the center of situations. You prefer to guide individuals in the "right" direction. You are a key observer of what is needed for yourself and others to achieve greatness.

Influential words:

Skillful

Focus

Greatness

Abilities and talents:

You are able to keep others in rhythm and headed in the "right" direction

You are able to guide situations in running smoothly

You are able to see the big picture and all the little steps it takes to complete it

Consciously experiencing this Language:

Knowing how to bring out your own greatness

Being in balance and harmony for yourself

Being comfortable in the spotlight as the center of focus

Being in the spotlight with grace and without ego

Accepting where you and others are on the journey

Knowing what steps are needed to complete your big vision

Unconsciously experiencing this Language:

Judging or demanding too much of yourself and others

Creating drama in order to be center-stage

Operating from a place of control instead of trust

Feeling as if you don't know which direction to take for yourself

Attracting individuals that are filled with drama

Creating situations that are full of struggle

Signs you are on the path:

You know which direction to take for yourself

You are balanced

You accept your role in the spotlight with grace

Language Orientation:

The *Ringmaster* is Action. Your Soul prefers to move directly into action. It is important that you pause to understand Divinely inspired action.

Accessing and Attracting Support:

Politician (Axiom of Quest) – These individuals provide sacred space for the truth. They can help the *Ringmaster* understand the truth inside of them to "see" their greatness more easily.

Huntress/Hunter (Axiom of Translation) – These individuals can help the *Ringmaster* understand what path the thing they desire will take.

Connoisseur (Tone) – These individuals are all about acceptance. They can help the *Ringmaster* accept themselves and others more fully.

IF YOUR BUSINESS'S TONE IS RINGMASTER:

You are clear about what direction you are taking clients in

You are clear in communicating the big vision to your clients

You accept your company's role as a leader in the spotlight

A CHILD WHO SPEAKS THIS LANGUAGE WILL THRIVE IN AN ENVIRONMENT THAT:

Provides them with a healthy desire to be in the spotlight

Provides them with a healthy respect for their own greatness, and the greatness of others

Provides them with opportunities to step into the spotlight and "run the show"

QUESTIONS TO ASK YOUR RINGMASTER:

How am I creating drama in this situation?

What is my greatness?

Sentinel

Tone

You prefer to go through life observing and keeping watch over others. Because you study situations closely, you have a keen understanding of what action is required and when.

By watching and guarding situations, you know when a path has ended and when to move on to a new situation.

INFLUENTIAL WORDS:

Guard

Divine Action

Support

ABILITIES AND TALENTS:

You are able to monitor and relay information precisely

You know what Divine action to take in order to resolve a situation

CONSCIOUSLY EXPERIENCING THIS LANGUAGE:

Watching and participating in your own life

Understanding when action is required, and moving forward with love and compassion

Knowing which situations truly require your involvement, and which do not

Providing guidance to others with love and compassion, not force or attachment

Being balanced in giving and receiving

Knowing that you are a support for others and allowing yourself to receive support

Experiencing Divine flow

Trusting that you are taking the right Divine action

UNCONSCIOUSLY EXPERIENCING THIS LANGUAGE:

Monitoring only, not engaging through Divinely inspired action

Feeling alienated and alone

Providing support in a co-dependent way

Guarding individuals without their consent

Resisting change

Being afraid to "make a move"

SIGNS YOU ARE ON THE PATH:

You know what Divine action to take for yourself

You are participating in your own life

You are creating Divine support for yourself and for others

LANGUAGE ORIENTATION:

The *Sentinel* is Action/Still. It is important to pause and check in with yourself and the Divine before taking action. This will allow for more Divinely inspired action and less struggle.

ACCESSING AND ATTRACTING SUPPORT:

Politician (Axiom of Quest) – These individuals provide a sacred space for others to speak their truth. They can provide the *Sentinel* with a place to feel safe communicating their observations.

Teacher (Axiom of Translation) – These individuals take complex subjects and present them in a way that others can understand. They can provide the *Sentinel* with knowledge to help them fully understand what they are observing.

Conductor (Tone) – These individuals prefer to bring out the best in others. They can help the *Sentinel* work within a group structure.

IF YOUR BUSINESS'S TONE IS SENTINEL:

You need to understand what the company watches and guards (a thought, a feeling, a space for others to be true to themselves, etc.)

You need to set up trustworthy relationships for the company

You need to set up structures for both strategy and action

A CHILD WHO SPEAKS THIS LANGUAGE WILL THRIVE IN AN ENVIRONMENT THAT:

Provides them with an understanding of when to take action

Provides them with an understanding of asking "permission" prior to taking action for someone else

Provides them with a structure to feel safe and to trust their instincts

QUESTIONS TO ASK YOUR SENTINEL:

Am I experiencing a lack of trust with myself and the Universe in this situation?

Am I afraid to take Divine action and, if so, why?

SHEPHERD

Tone

You prefer to go through life guiding and keeping watch over others.

You prefer to lead by example through actions and words. You are able to lead people with various backgrounds, interests, and ideologies.

All of your "followers" share a common destination. Most often the common destination of a *Shepherd's* flock is peace and balance within.

INFLUENTIAL WORDS:

Guide

Tranquility

Gather

ABILITIES AND TALENTS:

You are able to guide yourself and others to peace

You are listening to Divine guidance, guiding yourself and others to peace

CONSCIOUSLY EXPERIENCING THIS LANGUAGE:

Understanding that your role is to help others reach their destination of peace

Understanding that everyone has their own path

Knowing which situations truly involve you, and which do not

Guiding others with compassion and unconditional love

Understanding that you are a guide to peace, not its source

Being balanced within

Expressing peaceful words and actions

UNCONSCIOUSLY EXPERIENCING THIS LANGUAGE:

Attempting to push or pull others into your own idea of peace

Feeling impatient with your pace or the pace of others

Operating from a place of will or self-righteousness

Guiding by force

Looking outside for peace instead of within

SIGNS YOU ARE ON THE PATH:

You feel deeply connected to the Divine

You are operating from Divine love and support

You have created peace within

LANGUAGE ORIENTATION:

The *Shepherd* is Still. It is important that you feel connected to the Divine. Connection requires stillness. With this connection, you can guide through spirit and unconditional love.

ACCESSING AND ATTRACTING SUPPORT:

Negotiator (Axiom of Quest) – The *Negotiator's* mission is to help others create win/win deals. They can help the *Shepherd* see all sides of a situation.

Master (Axiom of Translation) – These individuals see the big picture. They can help the *Shepherd* see the larger vision of their life and the lives of others.

Disillusionist (Tone) – These individuals prefer to break down the illusions of a person's reality. They can help the *Shepherd* to stay focused on the Divine instead of the ego.

Also see the *Guardian* (Tone), page 363.

IF YOUR BUSINESS'S TONE IS SHEPHERD:

You need to understand what the company watches and protects

You need to understand how the company is guiding others to peace

You need to understand that clients will come and go as they reach their peace

A CHILD WHO SPEAKS THIS LANGUAGE WILL THRIVE IN AN ENVIRONMENT THAT:

Provides them with an understanding of how to lead peacefully

Provides them with love and support

Provides them with tools to operate from Divine love instead of ego

QUESTIONS TO ASK YOUR SHEPHERD:

Where in my life can I operate more from a place of Divine love?

Where am I listening to ego instead of Divine love?

SOOTHSAYER

Tone

You prefer to recognize and speak Divine truth. You have an understanding of future situations through the help of the Divine. You understand that choices are always being made and you can share the possibilities available when Soulful choices are made.

You understand that time is a human creation and everything is happening at once.

You are able to see and speak the truth. You forecast the future based upon Source information rather than scientific facts.

INFLUENTIAL WORDS:

See

Relay

Divine

ABILITIES AND TALENTS:

You are able to see and speak Divine truth

You are able to anticipate future events based on Divine information

CONSCIOUSLY EXPERIENCING THIS LANGUAGE:

Relaying information without attachment

Utilizing Divine voice

Living in the present while being able to see the past and the future

Knowing that the future is always changing based on the decisions we are making in the present

Being clear about your own future and which Divinely inspired actions to take

UNCONSCIOUSLY EXPERIENCING THIS LANGUAGE:

Inserting personal beliefs into your visions

Using your visions to influence others

Being unclear about your own future

Not living in the present

Feeling like your vision is cloudy

SIGNS YOU ARE ON THE PATH:

You are accessing and listening to Divine voice

You are living in the present

You are without attachment to the meaning of your visions

LANGUAGE ORIENTATION:

The *Soothsayer* is Still. Your Soul has a preference for reflection. Pausing and listening to your Soul will allow you to create a deeper connection with the Divine for clearer visions.

ACCESSING AND ATTRACTING SUPPORT:

Negotiator (Axiom of Quest) – These individuals help create new sustainable situations for themselves and others. They can help the *Soothsayer* understand where they are creating situations that are based on control.

Motivator (Axiom of Translation) – These individuals help motivate others to take a leap of faith. They can help the *Soothsayer* understand when they are being motivated by fear, which leads to unstable visions.

Connoisseur (Tone) – These individuals are about acceptance. They can help the *Soothsayer* love and accept themselves more fully.

IF YOUR BUSINESS'S TONE IS SOOTHSAYER:

You are clear about the truth and vision your company is offering

You create appropriate strategies for both the present and the future

You are flexible to changes in the vision

A CHILD WHO SPEAKS THIS LANGUAGE WILL THRIVE IN AN ENVIRONMENT THAT:

Provides them with opportunities to convey what they feel and to speak their truth

Provides them with opportunities to express what they are sensing

Provides them with a healthy outlook on the past, present, and future

QUESTIONS TO ASK YOUR SOOTHSAYER:

What am I attached to in this situation which is clouding my vision?

How can I live more in the present?

SOVEREIGN

Tone

You prefer to feel and express your innate sacred power. You prefer to utilize the force within you to create a life of ease.

The *Sovereign* prefers to lead by example and will be an individual that "takes the high road" through life.

INFLUENTIAL WORDS:

Divine

Power

Lead

ABILITIES AND TALENTS:

You are able to easily create your outer world from within

You are able to access your Divine power with ease and grace

CONSCIOUSLY EXPERIENCING THIS LANGUAGE:

Understanding that everyone has access to the same amount of power

Leading others to empowerment through love, compassion, and grace

Utilizing the Divine within for a life of ease and grace, for yourself and for others

Knowing that ultimate power comes from within

UNCONSCIOUSLY EXPERIENCING THIS LANGUAGE:

Using your power inappropriately

Being filled with worry, doubt, or fear

Believing that might is right

Feeling separate and divided

Losing faith

Feeling powerless

SIGNS YOU ARE ON THE PATH:

You know the source of your power

You feel complete and whole

You are leading with compassion and love

LANGUAGE ORIENTATION:

The *Sovereign* is Action. Your Soul has a preference to move directly into action. This can sometimes cause you to rush into decisions. Remember to allow yourself to move based on Divine inspiration.

ACCESSING AND ATTRACTING SUPPORT:

Prophet (Axiom of Quest) – These individuals not only understand a message, they know how to deliver it. They can help the *Sovereign* be a better leader.

Partner (Axiom of Translation) – These individuals are about creating true partnerships. They can help the *Sovereign* create supportive and sustainable partnerships.

Deliberator (Tone) – These individuals prefer to weigh all the pros and cons before making a decision. They can help the *Sovereign* make better choices and not rush into action.

IF YOUR BUSINESS'S TONE IS SOVEREIGN:

You are clear about what the company's power is, and you express it clearly

The company has an acknowledged leadership role

The company has a comprehensible way of supporting others within its own industry and in other industries

A CHILD WHO SPEAKS THIS LANGUAGE WILL THRIVE IN AN ENVIRONMENT THAT:

Provides them with tools to utilize their power appropriately

Provides them with opportunities to lead

Provides them with ways to tap into their own strength

QUESTIONS TO ASK YOUR SOVEREIGN:

How can I feel my true source of power more fully?

How can I lead more from a place of love and compassion?

SPEAKER OF GOD

Tone

You prefer to infuse a spiritual imprint into your daily speech and every aspect of your daily life.

You innately understand the power of the spoken word and how it can be utilized to bring unification to all.

When using the Language unconsciously, the *Speaker of God* may speak carelessly and withhold Love from themselves or others.

INFLUENTIAL WORDS:

Divine

Love

Word(s)

ABILITIES AND TALENTS:

You are able to share the Divine via the spoken word

You are able to encode every word with the imprint of love

CONSCIOUSLY EXPERIENCING THIS LANGUAGE:

Focusing on messages of unity, wholeness, and love for yourself and others

Feeling complete and whole

Feeling supported by and connected to the Divine

Incorporating the Divine into every aspect of your life

"Speaking" your Divine truth

Understanding that we are all one

Understanding that we all are able to speak with Divine voice

UNCONSCIOUSLY EXPERIENCING THIS LANGUAGE:

"Speaking" carelessly

Withholding love from yourself or others

Feeling separate from the Divine

Feeling unsupported by the Divine

Being afraid of your connection to the Divine

Utilizing the Divine to separate yourself from others

SIGNS YOU ARE ON THE PATH:

You are full of love and compassion for yourself

You have a deep connection and relationship with the Divine

You are unafraid to discuss the Divine in a way that is appropriate for you in your everyday life

LANGUAGE ORIENTATION:

The *Speaker of God* is Still. Your Soul prefers to reflect. It is important that you allow yourself time to connect to and deepen your relationship with the Divine.

ACCESSING AND ATTRACTING SUPPORT:

Observer (Axiom of Quest) – These individuals are able to see all. They can help the *Speaker of God* see all the facts of a situation.

Lawmaker (Axiom of Translation) – These individuals create structures for peace. They can help the *Speaker of God* create beliefs that support safety and internal peace.

Conductor (Tone) – These individuals highlight the best in everyone within a group. They are born leaders and can help the *Speaker of God* be a better leader.

IF YOUR BUSINESS'S TONE IS SPEAKER OF GOD:

You are clear about what the company's Divine truth is and you communicate it clearly

You provide opportunities for the company to take a leadership role for truth

You have in place structures for all to speak their spiritual truths

A CHILD WHO SPEAKS THIS LANGUAGE WILL THRIVE IN AN ENVIRONMENT THAT:

Provides them with opportunities to speak their truth

Allows them to determine their own spiritual path

Provides them with opportunities to express love and compassion

QUESTIONS TO ASK YOUR SPEAKER OF GOD:

Why am I afraid to speak my Divine truth?

How can I bring more awareness of the Divine into my daily life?

SPRINTER

Tone

You prefer to move rapidly from one thing to the next: a project, an idea, a location, a situation, etc.

It is easy for you to "see the end of things." Timing is an important concept for you.

It is important for you to work within time, not outside it. For example, in order to avoid feeling frustrated, you need to be patient and understand that timing is a component of manifestation. Be willing to release frustration and life will flow more easily.

INFLUENTIAL WORDS:

Quick

Conclusion

Time

ABILITIES AND TALENTS:

You are able to move quickly from one situation, event, or project to the next

You are able to "see the finish line"

You are able to work with time in ways that others cannot

CONSCIOUSLY EXPERIENCING THIS LANGUAGE:

Being able to move through activities with ease and grace

Feeling compassion for yourself and others

Being without attachment to your own pace or the pace of others

Living in the present

Having a clear sense of the finish line and yet being able to make adjustments and be flexible

Being balanced between action and stillness

Unconsciously experiencing this Language:

Becoming frustrated or angry when things are not moving quickly

Being frustrated or angry that others cannot "see the finish line"

Racing through life, not being able to witness and participate in all of the miracles and guidance that are being provided for you

Signs you are on the path:

You are creating a balanced pace

You are in Divine flow, moving through action with grace and ease

You are full of love and compassion for yourself and others, especially those who can't "see the finish line"

Language Orientation:

The *Sprinter* is Action/Still. Your Soul prefers to reflect and then move into Divinely inspired action. This will help you move swiftly and accurately.

Accessing and Attracting Support:

Mentor (Axiom of Quest) – These individuals are about guiding others. They can provide the *Sprinter* with guidance on how to be balanced.

Image Maker (Axiom of Translation) – These individuals see the essence of a being and then help bring that essence into reality. They can help the *Sprinter* understand what is driving them to the finish line.

Carter (Tone) – These individuals express a certain message for themselves and others. They can help the *Sprinter* understand what they are carrying around that is slowing them down.

IF YOUR BUSINESS'S TONE IS SPRINTER:

You are clear about what steps need to be taken and the timing of those steps

You provide a structure and plan to provide a clear pace for your clients

You have incorporated planning time into the business plan in order to keep a balanced pace for growth

A CHILD WHO SPEAKS THIS LANGUAGE WILL THRIVE IN AN ENVIRONMENT THAT:

Provides them with a balanced pace for action

Provides them with opportunities to explain how they see the outcome of a situation

Provides them with compassion and respect for their abilities, and for the abilities of others

QUESTIONS TO ASK YOUR SPRINTER:

Where am I moving too fast?

What attachment do I have to what I think is the finish line?

STABILIZER

Tone

You prefer to provide stabilization for many circumstances and people.

You recognize that interactions can involve conflict and you are skilled at preventing potential instability in situations.

INFLUENTIAL WORDS:

Stable

Structure

Steady

ABILITIES AND TALENTS:

You offer a sense of support to create a more stable environment

You are able to diffuse situations to avoid conflict

Your energy can help decrease or eliminate the chance that a situation will deteriorate

CONSCIOUSLY EXPERIENCING THIS LANGUAGE:

Being in unconditional love for yourself

Being neutral in situations, providing others the opportunity to see their own misperceptions

Maintaining your own stability

Understanding where your own beliefs, structure, etc. need to be reinforced to keep you stable

Having the internal wisdom and strength to stand out without feeling insecure or threatened

UNCONSCIOUSLY EXPERIENCING THIS LANGUAGE:

Imposing your viewpoint on others

Being overcome by a fear of "not being safe"

Feeling unstable

Being part of the problem instead of the solution

Creating co-dependent relationships based on needing safety

SIGNS YOU ARE ON THE PATH:

You feel a sense of safety inside of you

You understand when to be firm and when to be flexible

You are full of unconditional love for yourself and turn to that for stability

LANGUAGE ORIENTATION:

The *Stabilizer* is Still. Your Soul prefers to reflect. This is important in order to feel true safety and stability.

ACCESSING AND ATTRACTING SUPPORT:

Negotiator (Axiom of Quest) – The *Negotiator's* mission is to help create new, sustainable deals. They can help the *Stabilizer* create new arrangements of true support.

Purveyor (Axiom of Translation) – These individuals have access to an unlimited supply of resources. They can help the *Stabilizer* find support for themselves and others.

Disillusionist (Tone) – These individuals break down illusions and help create more sustainable support. They can help the *Stabilizer* understand where they have beliefs that are creating instability.

IF YOUR BUSINESS'S TONE IS STABILIZER:

You are clear about what support you offer to your clients

You have clear structures in place so the business feels supported and stable

You have a clear understanding of how the company wishes to be "out in front" and have created a safe structure for it to embrace that role

A CHILD WHO SPEAKS THIS LANGUAGE WILL THRIVE IN AN ENVIRONMENT THAT:

Provides them with a sense that they are safe

Provides them with appropriate boundaries

Supports them in developing a strong sense of self

QUESTIONS TO ASK YOUR STABILIZER:

Where and why do I feel unstable?

Where am I acting as a source of safety in a way that is not supportive for myself and others?

Synergist

Tone

You have an innate knowing of how events, people, and situations are meaningfully related.

You are able to quickly move past limiting beliefs that keep you from being part of the flow.

You understand that working with the energetic flow is more efficient than trying to control it.

Influential words:

Synchronicity

Flow

Current

Abilities and talents:

You are able to understand all the related parts of situations or events

You are able to step into synchronicity easily and gracefully

You easily understand what "elements" can be merged to create more efficient flow

Consciously experiencing this Language:

Easily seeing and knowing the meaning in seemingly random events

Easily moving through any beliefs that prevent you from living in synchronicity

Allowing yourself to be guided into the flow

Moving from one event to the next in synchronicity

UNCONSCIOUSLY EXPERIENCING THIS LANGUAGE:

Living in fear, especially of losing control

Trying to control the flow

Feeling unsupported

Feeling that everything is just random

Struggling

SIGNS YOU ARE ON THE PATH:

You feel one with the flow

You understand the events that are happening and why

You are living in synchronicity

LANGUAGE ORIENTATION:

The *Synergist* is Action/Still. Your Soul requires reflection to follow Divine action and be in the flow with the Universe.

ACCESSING AND ATTRACTING SUPPORT:

Negotiator (Axiom of Quest) – The *Negotiator's* mission is to help create new sustainable deals. They can help the *Synergist* understand where they are engaged in co-creative "deals" with the Universe and where they are trying to control.

Motivator (Axiom of Translation) – These individuals understand motivation. They can help the *Synergist* understand what is motivating them, whether fear or love.

Connoisseur (Tone) – These individuals are about acceptance. They can help the *Synergist* understand where they need to accept and love themselves more fully. This will help with being in Divine flow.

IF YOUR BUSINESS'S TONE IS SYNERGIST:

You are clear how you are helping your clients be in the flow

You have a structure in place to express and create flow for the company

You are clear on what offer you provide for your clients to feel safe allowing the flow

A CHILD WHO SPEAKS THIS LANGUAGE WILL THRIVE IN AN ENVIRONMENT THAT:

Provides them with a sense of safety and trust

Provides them with support in experiencing the flow of the Universe

Provides them with the ability both to be guided and to lead

QUESTIONS TO ASK YOUR SYNERGIST:

What am I trying to control in this situation and why?

Where in my life do I feel unsupported and why?

WEAVER

Tone

You bring together several different Divine voices into one. You can easily speak and express how things "fit together" to create a larger tapestry. You understand that the Divine speaks with many voices but always the same message.

You offer richness in bringing together many voices and visions, assembling them like a tapestry of life. You understand that differences can co-exist with similarities in a way that brings all parties together for the greater good.

INFLUENTIAL WORDS:

Together

Divine

One

ABILITIES AND TALENTS:

You are able to assemble different ideas so they complement each other

You are able to understand the advantages of many voices with one message

CONSCIOUSLY EXPERIENCING THIS LANGUAGE:

Weaving together, without attachment, a myriad of ideas to show the larger picture

Feeling part of the whole

Knowing that you are complete and whole

Knowing and understanding the big tapestry of Divine wisdom

Unconsciously experiencing this Language:

Feeling alone and separate

Feeling frustrated when others cannot recognize wisdom

Feeling as if you are only seeing half of the picture

Feeling a sense of failure when you cannot weave everyone into the big tapestry

Signs you are on the path:

You know your own voice

You understand your place within the group

You bring many voices together without feeling lost or alone

Language Orientation:

The *Weaver* is Still. Your Soul requires reflection. This will allow you to understand how information, people, etc. fit into the big picture or tapestry.

Accessing and Attracting Support:

Prophet (Axiom of Quest) – The *Prophet's* mission is about having a message and a delivery system for that message. They can help the *Weaver* understand messages that bring us all together.

Motivator (Axiom of Translation) – These individuals understand motivation. They can help the *Weaver* understand what is motivating them, whether fear or love.

Collaborator (Tone) – These individuals are all about co-creating with themselves and others. They can help the *Weaver* with their own collaborations in order to create a stronger tapestry for themselves and others.

IF YOUR BUSINESS'S TONE IS WEAVER:

> Your are clear what ideas you are weaving together for clients
>
> You have a community and a place in the community
>
> You provide the "big picture" for the company, its employees, and its clients

A CHILD WHO SPEAKS THIS LANGUAGE WILL THRIVE IN AN ENVIRONMENT THAT:

> Supports them in understanding that we are all one
>
> Allows them to share their big vision
>
> Provides them with opportunities to express their thoughts and ideas

QUESTIONS TO ASK YOUR WEAVER:

> Why am I feeling alone and separate?
>
> What wisdom do I have that I need to hear myself?

PART THREE

Becoming More Conscious

CHAPTER 8:

Integrating Soul Language

You will learn in this chapter:

- How Soul Languages can be amplified

- Going deeper in your journey

- Answers to frequently asked questions

Understanding your Languages is only the first step in creating a deeper connection with your Soul and your Higher Power. The second step is conversation; ideally, you will want to create a conscious connection between you and your Soul (via your Soul Language team) daily.

Like any tool to support your evolutionary process, being consistent about your connection allows you to keep turning and focusing on the "big truths."

When we are hitting on something big in our life, there are all sorts of ways that ego will distract us to keep us in our old "safe" patterns. These are bumps in the road and Soul Language is a process to help you understand how you are still on the road despite those bumps. It is a way to access support as you continue on your powerful journey.

And, when you are ready, there are also other ways to connect to yourself and the world around you in deeper ways using Soul Language.

Amplification

When you meet someone who speaks the same Language as you, you each serve to amplify the other's energy and power.

Amplification means that when two or more Soul Language members (people who share the same Soul Language) gather, they create a cone of intensity. This cone or power structure can then be utilized to help people on their paths.

Like all of Soul Language, there is a conscious amplification and an unconscious amplification.

Amplification of the Axiom of Quest:

A conscious amplification of one's Axiom of Quest will be expressed as an attraction of additional resources, tools, and individuals so the shared mission can be enjoyed without struggle.

When consciously being in mission together, the shared mission can be instantly revealed in a deeper, bigger way. An amplification will also facilitate the manifestation of carrying out the mission.

An unconscious amplification of one's Axiom of Quest will be expressed as a need to fulfill or complete the shared mission. This can bring up feelings of being "not good enough."

An unconscious amplification can also amplify any misalignments in the individuals. For example, if both of the Soul Language members have a failure trigger, the amplification can intensify that trigger. This can result in a release of that fear (conscious amplification) or an explosion or implosion of that fear (unconscious amplification).

Amplification of the Axiom of Translation:

A conscious amplification of one's Axiom of Translation will be expressed as an affirmation of movement in the mission. Each individual will experience situations that multiply the fuel of the mission.

An unconscious amplification of one's Axiom of Translation will be expressed as a lack of fuel. The individuals will feel as if there is no movement in their life or in their mission.

Amplification of the Tone:

A conscious amplification of one's Tone will be expressed as increased support for free-will choices that benefit the Soul's agenda.

An unconscious amplification of one's Tone will be expressed as ego running the show and decisions being made through the filter of the ego.

Going Deeper in Your Journey

As you go deeper in your journey, your ego or mind may feel 'threatened' and come up with ways to distract you. Your mind is a part of you; it is not our goal to be at war with the ego, but to love this part of you for trying to keep you in the illusion of safety by keeping to your patterns.

That being said, it is important is to have an awareness of how your ego is distracting you. Below are several examples:

"It's Not Working" or "I'm Not Getting Anything"–It is possible that Soul Language doesn't resonate with you. Much more likely is that ego is playing the "it's not working" game. We live in a world used to instant gratification. Transformation isn't always instant. Allow yourself the time to integrate Soulful information. Also, ask yourself this question: "Is it not working because I'm not keeping my commitment with myself?" Remember, Soul Language is a spiritual process and not an intellectual one.

"I Don't Have Time"–Scarcity is a big weapon of the ego. Not enough time, money, etc. There is always enough. How much time do you think it takes to connect with your Soul? How much time are you going to give yourself? Do you have five minutes to start? Connect for five minutes a day for 10 days and then assess the situation again.

"Why Am I Not Like…"–When you compare yourself with another person, ego is in charge and you can expect to feel frustration. We all have the same amount of power. If you like the way someone is using their power, take the time to model it.

"I Have Already Worked On That"–This is ego at its highest. There are several big themes in life. We each have one (or more) big challenges that are going to come up again and again. This is a good thing (I know it doesn't sound like it, but it is!) because it gives you a chance to love yourself more and bring yourself closer to the Divine. I don't know anyone who doesn't desire those two things.

"I'm Not Accomplishing Anything"–One of my personal favorites. We tend to believe that if we are not creating movement then movement isn't happening. There is a lot going on behind the scenes. This is ego's way of taking advantage of your lack of trust. When I feel like that, I take a deep breath and set the intention that I will KNOW when it is time to take Divine action.

"It's Not Meant To Be"–I believe this phrase was created to support individuals and give them comfort, but ego has twisted it. It can be used as an excuse. We are creators of our own world—if you desire it, it is meant to be.

"It Can't Be That Easy"—Yes, it is as easy as listening to your Soul. The part that requires some effort is what you do with that information, how you react. This is your chance to be in the world, the way your Soul knows you can be.

FREQUENTLY ASKED QUESTIONS

Q: What is a Soul Language Identification session?

A: According to the information I have received, there are 107 individual Soul Languages. Each and every person has three Soul Languages that he or she speaks. They are broken down into three different categories: Axiom of Quest, Axiom of Translation, and Tone.

Axiom of Quest: Your mission, your path, the reason why you are on this planet at this time

Axiom of Translation: How you will be known here, the fuel of your mission

Tone: Your Soulful personality

During a Soul Language Identification session, your three Soul Languages are revealed via muscle testing or kinesiology—a tool that allows us to quickly and accurately tap into the body's innate knowledge.

After your three individual Soul Languages are revealed to you, the practitioner can help you to understand how those three Languages shape your life. They can also help guide you in understanding how you might be consciously or unconsciously using those Languages.

Q: Do I need to know how to muscle test?

A: No, a Soul Language Practitioner will ask your permission before the session begins, and will use their body to connect with your Soul and receive a response from your body.

Q: How was Soul Language created?

A: The information was received via Divine guidance. Several years ago I was at a conference, looking around at the other attendees and wondering why I connected instantly with some but didn't feel compelled to speak to others. I asked the Universe, "How can I attract more people like these?" The answer I received was, "You speak the same language."

That answer led to the paradigm of Soul Language. Since then I have been actively developing and refining the practice.

Q: Do your Soul Languages ever change?

A: No. Think of them like the fingerprints of your Soul.

Q: Can you conduct a Soul Language session over the phone?

A: Yes. In fact, most identification sessions have happened by phone. Think of humans as energy points on a big grid. All it takes is to focus on that energy point.

Q: What do I need to do to prepare for a session with a Soul Language Practitioner?

A: It is suggested that you come prepared for the phone or in-person session with a couple questions for which you would like insight or guidance.

Q: What might I expect from a session?

A: During a session, you can expect insight and guidance on issues you are dealing with, plus tools and resources to help create a shift. This will help you achieve maximum results in your life.

Q: What sorts of clients use Soul Language?

Soul Language attracts people who want to know their purpose, who are done playing small or pretending and are ready to put themselves out there. We work with business leaders and a lot of individuals in transition. We also teach group classes, work with coaches who have private clients, and work with metaphysical coaches and transformational leaders.

Q: How can Soul Language help me at work?

A: By understanding your Soul Languages, you will be able to work better with your team. You'll find it easier to communicate, and work will get done more easily and effectively. If you're a manager or business owner you can learn to become a better leader, and if you're a leader in training you will gain important insights that can help you achieve your goals.

Q: How can Soul Language help me in my relationships and family life?

A: Relationships fail, whether romantic or a business relationships, for usually the same reasons. Either we conduct most of the relationship with that other person in our heads, or we don't ask for want we want and spend half the time not being ourselves. Soul Language provides tools for obtaining the best possible relationships in all kinds of situations.

By learning about your own Soul Languages, and the Soul Languages of others, you can understand each other better and know what you can count on each other for. You won't ask yourself "Why does this person keep acting that way?" and you'll be able to better communicate honestly and openly to build the relationships that you really want.

Q: What does an intuitive healer do?

A: An intuitive healer works with the spirit and nature to provide insight, guidance, and healing for others.

Q: What does being "intuitive" mean?

A: Being intuitive means listening to the inner knowledge or "gut feelings." As an intuitive for others I sense their inner guidance and connect with that in order to provide insight. Sometimes it feels like plucking an idea out of the air, sometimes I see words on a blackboard, at other times I see an image.

Q: Will knowing my Soul Language help me find my Soulmate?

A: Yes, because when you love and accept yourself fully and completely, you naturally attract others who love and accept you fully.

Q: Do animals have Soul Languages?

A: Yes. Everything with an essence and a Soul has Soul Languages. While animals do have a Soul, however, they do not have free-will. Animals reflect parts of their owners. Understanding your pet's Soul Languages will allow you to enjoy a more conscious relationship (connection).

Q: Can I learn how to use my intuitive abilities?

A: Yes. We all have intuitive abilities. Some of us just work that muscle more than others. To start working your own intuitive muscle you need to set your intention to be more aware of your inner guidance system. Group classes and one-on-one sessions on this topic are also available.

CHAPTER 9:

The Soul Language Community

You will learn in this chapter:

- How people are using Soul Language

- How to get more involved with the Soul Language community

Receiving Community

Recently it has become even more apparent how important community is in our lives, in our evolution and in nurturing our Souls.

One of the reasons I believe I received this information is that the question I asked was about receiving community in my life. I wanted to be surrounded by like-minded individuals and I wanted to support people who were interested in being closer to the Divine.

What has happened of course has been bigger than my wildest dreams. When individuals connect with each other based on this understanding of Soul Language, there exists a profound connection, a willingness to support each other, and a deep understanding that I haven't experienced in other areas of my life.

As the Soul Language community grows, we continue to see lasting connections being formed organically between members of the community. As we grow in consciousness and embrace the concept that we are all one, the community will be an ongoing resource to support that understanding.

If you find yourself attracted to a particular person, it may be that they have something to offer you. Or they could share a Language with someone you love and trust. Keep in mind that just because someone shares a Soul Language with a person you love and trust, that does not automatically make them trustworthy.

You also may notice particular Languages that you bump heads with. It might be that there is an unresolved conflict with someone who "speaks" that same Soul Language. Once you find resolution with that person, you might find it easier to get along with others who share their Soul Language.

By learning the Soul Languages of others in your life, you are able to see what Languages you attract and what Languages are attracted to you.

How People are Using Soul Language

The one question I receive a lot, which seems appropriate to include at the end of the book, is this:

How are people using Soul Language?

This is a very expansive question. I can only talk about what I have experienced, and share what others have told me about their experiences. Individuals are using Soul Language to:

- Communicate clearly about themselves
- Connect more deeply with their children, partners, and mates
- Connect with themselves and the Divine, to remember their truth and to experience peace
- Accept and move into the consciousness of love
- Remember who they are and express themselves fully
- Speak their truth and create from that place

Business owners are using Soul Language to:

- Align with the mission of their business
- Create more powerful and productive teams
- Craft their elevator speeches
- Communicate from the heart and let go of marketing from pain or fear

Healers are using Soul Language to help their clients create a deeper sense of safety. Personal coaches, life coaches, business coaches and executive coaches are all using Soul Language to fuel their own missions and help their clients gain a greater sense of clarity and purpose.

How to Get Involved

Once you understand more about your Soul, it is a natural progression to want to understand more about the other Souls in your life. We have created several ways to support you with creating a fully conscious life.

Business Soul Language Identification

This is where the three Soul Languages of your business are identified and you discuss the conscious and unconscious use of these languages with a Soul Language Practitioner. You also learn how you are impacting your business, all based on how you are utilizing your personal Soul Languages in relationship to the business.

Having the Soul Languages of your business identified gives you a tool you can work with on a daily basis. Through understanding these three Languages, you can create a conscious connection between your Soul and the Soul of your business (via your Soul Language team). This will support you in working more consciously, attracting appropriate team members, and achieving your goals.

You will have the tools to:

- Understand and attract your community in a bigger way
- Operate based on your own definition of success
- Understand that it is your right to thrive and excel
- Embrace your talents and the talents and gifts of the business
- Move into action and take this knowledge to the next level

Sacred Partnership Soul Language Identification

This is where the Soul Languages of your business partnership, marriage, joint venture, family union, etc. are identified. A Soul Language Practitioner discusses with each partner how their personal Languages impact the conscious and unconscious energy within that partnership.

Couples Soul Language Identification

Soul Language is an amazing tool for creating a conscious connection between you and your Soul, so you have a deep understanding of your mission and the talents you draw on to fuel that mission. When you identify your Soul Languages, it is like opening up a book and reading all about yourself. Imagine having that same knowledge about your life partner. How would this information impact the way you relate to one another?

By having your Soul Languages identified, you and your partner will have the opportunity to:

- Gain profound insight about each other
- Understand what each of you needs in order to feel loved, accepted, and supported
- Experience a deep sense of acceptance about your own and your partner's unique nature
- Strengthen your connection with each other
- Improve communication
- Have a deeper level of compassion for yourself and for your partner
- Experience a deeper clarity about why you were brought together

Family Soul Language Identification

Our family dynamics shape so much in our lives. They shape our definitions of love and self-worth. They influence our relationship with the Divine. They set up our fears and our beliefs.

By knowing the Soul Languages of your family members, you will have the opportunity to:

- Gain profound insight about each child
- Understand how to provide an environment where every family member feels loved, accepted, and supported
- Experience a deep sense of acceptance for each person's unique nature
- Strengthen your connection with each child
- Have a deeper level of compassion for yourself and for others
- Experience a deeper clarity about how to parent each child

We notice that there is relief and joy when a parent understands that they are a good parent and that, with a few tweaks, they can become a parent who nurtures their child's natural Soulful talents.

Soul Dates

Tap into the wisdom of the community by connecting with others who speak your Language(s), or ones you want to attract in order to learn from them. Thousands of people have had their Soul Languages identified and the community is continuously growing.

Where this is going

This whole paradigm explains why we jump into some things and not others. Why we trust some people and not others. Why we attract certain types of people and repel others. Why we have beautiful gifts to share but sometimes feel like nobody notices them.

We each have a role to play, and Soul Language helps us understand ours on a level that is deeper than the mind. This is not about changing your personality, or even building your strengths. This is about knowing who you are and discovering what it means to just be yourself with nothing in the way.

What a different world it will be as more and more people find their way to Soul Language. It has been a great honor to bring this forth and to play my own unique role in the birth of this amazing revolution, and I am grateful for the community's support for my own journey.

www.SoulLanguage.us